# Natural Born Winners

Robin Sieger is the founder of the Sieger Group, a consulting and corporate training organisation based in London. The company has built an international reputation amongst businesses and organisations as a powerful catalyst for performance transformation.

The Sieger Group works internationally, helping individuals and organisations release their potential through strategy innovations, breakthrough initiatives and the creation of an internal success culture, turning potential into progress. They have a wide range of clients – from start-up entrepreneurs through to FT-SE 100 companies.

In addition to the Sieger Group he holds non-executive directorships in several other companies, works with charities and develops educational programmes. He also runs the Natural Born Winners™ seminar for the public during the year.

A world class keynote speaker, he is noted for his humour and ability to inspire, motivate and transform corporate audiences internationally. His corporate training, consulting and speaking clients include Andersen Consulting, Blockbuster, British Aerospace, British Telecom, General Motors, Glaxo Wellcome, IBM, McDonalds, Microsoft and Toshiba.

GU00341823

# NATURAL BORN WINNERS

*How to Achieve Your Ambitions
and Create the Success You Want*

Robin Sieger

RANDOM HOUSE

BUSINESS BOOKS

Published in the United Kingdom in 2000 by
Random House Business Books

5 7 9 10 8 6

Copyright © Robin Sieger 1999

The right of Robin Sieger to be identified as the author of this work has
been asserted by him in accordance with the Copyright, Designs and
Patents Act, 1988

First published in the United Kingdom in 1999 by Century
This edition first published in 2000 by Arrow Books

Arrow Books
The Random House Group Limited
20 Vauxhall Bridge Road, London SW1V 2SA

Random House Australia (Pty) Limited
20 Alfred Street, Milsons Point, Sydney,
New South Wales 2061, Australia

Random House New Zealand Limited
18 Poland Road, Glenfield,
Auckland 10, New Zealand

Random House (Pty) Limited
Endulini, 5A Jubilee Road, Parktown 2193, South Africa

The Random House Group Limited Reg. No. 954009

www.randomhouse.co.uk

A CIP catalogue record for this book is available from the British Library

Papers used by Random House are natural, recyclable products made from
wood grown in sustainable forests. The manufacturing processes conform to
the environmental regulations of the country of origin.

Printed and bound in Denmark by
Nørhaven A/S, Viborg

ISBN 0 09 928093 0

# Contents

To my father
Dr A. E. Sieger
Who taught me to love, to laugh, and to play golf,
in that order.

# Introduction

Sometimes life can seem so unfair. You work hard, you do your best – but nothing seems to change. And yet there are others who, with the effortless ease of angels, always seem to get what they want. Why?

My father, a single-handed general practitioner in Glasgow, died at the age of fifty-two from a combination of overwork and stress. After a lifetime of dedication to his family and his patients, it seemed so unjust. And then, when I was only twenty-nine, and poised for the first time in my life to achieve a real degree of success, I was diagnosed with cancer. Talk about not getting a break.

Up until that point in my life I had vaguely hoped that I would be successful, that fate would deal me some luck and that I would enjoy a life of security and financial freedom. But curiously, although I knew my aspirations for the future required me to act, I didn't really believe it would make any difference whether I did or not. In other words, I felt my destiny was ultimately in somebody else's hands. So rather than going out to make the success I wanted happen, I was waiting for it to happen to me. The difference was crucial. In consequence, I lived at the time a life less than fully realised, suffering the silent rage of watching time pass me by, always ready to blame others or excuse myself – too willing to put my future on hold until something came along.

Even as a young boy I'd been the same. I'd wondered, like so many, what the future held for me. I'd wondered if I was going to fulfil my childhood dreams, whilst secretly believing I never would. That deep-bred belief in the inevitability of failure and disappointment was hard to shake. I went to an academic school believing I would fail: I was right. I even went to university believing I would fail – right again. These were truly self-fulfilling prophecies. But when occasionally I tried doing things at which I fundamentally believed I would succeed, the curious fact is that I did.

It was only after being diagnosed with cancer that I finally made the connection, that I got the wake-up call and in a moment of insight learned the lesson. That simple realisation was a life-changing experience for me, and one that has ultimately led to this book being written. It wasn't complicated or grandiose; I didn't unlock the secret of the universe, or discover a simple one-step method to instant happiness. But I did understand why winners win.

Over the next few years I read and studied everything I could and spoke to those whose experiences I could learn from. I distilled the recurring principles into a form I could make clear, simple, and put in to immediate effect. I understood that knowledge alone is not power; it needs to be properly applied for it to be truly powerful.

I began to use my knowledge and live my life in a more focused, positive manner, and the transformation was as dramatic as it was immediate and tangible. The anxiety and stress I had experienced in the past were replaced with strong feelings of confidence and peacefulness. I felt genuinely in step with life, or as I expressed it to a friend: 'at last the shoes fit perfectly'. My future was no longer a maze of uncertainties to be avoided but rather a journey of experiences to be embraced and enjoyed. I was happy.

As I reaped the personal and material benefits of my new philosophy I became full of enthusiasm for communicating it to others and helping them achieve success. I distilled the system into a two-day course that I called Natural Born Winners. Initially I ran the courses locally for free. Today the business has grown as I intended into one that develops the potential of individuals and organisations in the creation of success. We apply the

Natural Born Winners philosophy in training courses on leadership, change management, customer care and team work – in fact on all areas of business and life where the outcome will be directly affected more by how we *think* than by how we *work*.

I now lecture at conferences internationally, and I recognise that the components of success are universal, timeless and constant – and have little to do with its apparent trappings. Success is no more a matter of luck than winning is simply about coming first or happiness about having lots of money. We all recognise and understand the paradox that you can be rich and still be poor; that you can enjoy huge status and yet still be miserable.

Successful people and businesses are winners on the inside. Success is an internal feeling with external manifestations. It wasn't that in my researches I had discovered anything new, but it was that I had discovered it for myself. As I have sometimes joked, life comes without an instruction manual – and yet we are born with the innate abilities to overcome its challenges. The closest we have to a manual is to be located within ourselves. We've just forgotten it's there.

I have written this book in order to share with you knowledge that is timeless and constant, and to introduce you to a practical, easy to apply programme that will develop your winning potential.

I haven't climbed Mount Everest or won an Olympic gold, but my journey to understanding has been every bit as demanding. I have experienced the frustrations of com- placency and the anxiety of an uncertain future. Whatever frustrations you have experienced, be assured that I know where you're coming from.

Whoever you are, whatever your circumstances, this book is for you. I don't think of it as a self-help book. I regard it as more of a help-yourself book. Take from it those lessons that make sense and that you feel able to apply, and grow into the winner you were born to be. You can make a difference to your life if you apply the knowledge with understanding to create the future you want. It's rarely easy: you will need to stay the course with perseverance, commitment and determination. But you can do it.

I dearly wish I had known and understood as a young man the things I now know to be true. It's too easy to convince ourselves that we can't achieve the goals we set ourselves, that we cannot realise our dreams. It is my deepest wish that I may help you believe this: you can. Because I know that when you believe you can, you will.

# 1 Success

I remember sitting with a group of comedians in Los Angeles, all of them – like me – struggling hopefuls on the comedy circuit. I had taken myself there to learn all I could in a year by working in the most competitive market in the world. It was 1985 and comedy was the new rock 'n' roll: success meant wealth, fame, and the ability to jump the queue at any restaurant in town, plus fast cars, beautiful women, and a mansion in Beverly Hills. Such were the rewards we dreamed of, the Holy Grail we all aspired to.

I had been there for about six months and had slowly worked my way up the club circuit. No one was paying me yet, but at least I was working at weekends and there was always the possibility of being discovered – a possibility we all clung to. Of course, hardly anyone ever *was* discovered, so the usual thing after a show was for a bunch of us aspiring stars to head for some bar or diner where we would while away the hours before making our way home, carrying out en route critical a dissection of the relative merits of rival comedians. So on this particular occasion there I was at an all-night deli with a group of other comics, engaged in our favourite topic, when I began to notice that, almost without thinking, we were habitually dividing the comedians under discussion into two distinct categories. Those who were doing even less well than us we considered to have some talent – in varying amounts – but to be extremely unlikely ever to make it to the big time. Those who were obviously more successful than us, on the other hand, we mainly referred to as 'lucky'.

Luck, we felt, was the overriding, the determining factor, in success: luck, which might – or might not – at any time touch any one of us, in whatever guise. We all hoped that we had what it took to get to the top and we all hoped that luck would single us out. But we were wrong to look at success in this way. In fact the ones who *did* make it never just hoped – they believed. That was the difference between us. That was the difference between success and failure.

Since that evening I have been through a number of extraordinary experiences which have for ever changed my view of myself and of my potential. And many times subsequently in business and in client meetings, I heard people express limitless variations on those conversations I had in 1985 in Los Angeles.

One thing I know for sure. Success is *not* a matter of luck. Luck is a matter of random chance, while success is a matter of design.

**Success is a matter of luck. If you want proof, ask any failure.**

*Earl Wilson*

So if success is a matter of design, where's the blue-print?

The answer to that question has to begin with some understanding of what success means. If I were to ask you what you really want out of life, what would you tell me?

Money, fame and freedom, perhaps, at the personal level, just as many companies would wish for profit, growth and recognition.

` But does having money of itself make you successful? Surely not, or lottery winners, bank robbers and the heirs of great estates would automatically be considered great successes. What about fame? History demonstrates that fame is no guarantee of success or happiness, any more than the pursuit and realisation of personal freedom is.

I believe that the answer lies elsewhere, that success is

best defined as the gradual realisation of your goals, both personal and professional. Wealth, fame and the rest are simply by-products created by the achievement of these goals.

Ask a successful person what they want out of life and the answer won't be vague or sweeping: they will give you a clear definition of what success means to them, a clearly defined goal that they've reached or are still heading for. But that goal won't be a certain sum of money in the bank or a state of general happiness. It will be a very specific objective, the realisation of which will create the desired satisfaction.

This ability to define a goal is part of what makes winners win, whether at the individual or the business level. Winners have the same opportunities and disappointments as you and I. What distinguishes long-term winners is the way they think, and their attitude. And those are the only two things in life that everyone has absolute control over.

Success is not a matter of luck – it's a matter of design. Winners don't *get* more opportunities – they *create* them. They don't let setbacks reinforce a poor self-image; they see them as opportunities in disguise, as chances to bolster their resolve to succeed.

Whatever dream you have for your future, provided it is within the realms of the possible it is within the realms of the achievable. But the attainment of your goal will not be the result of reading a book (even this one) in the hope that it may reveal a hidden code or the framework for a get-rich-quick scheme. Because if you truly want your life to take the direction of success and happiness, you need to make a real commitment, create an unquenchable self-belief, feel a passion for what you are aiming for, and never ever take your eye off your goal.

**That man is a success who has lived well, laughed often and loved much.**
                                *Robert Louis Stevenson (1850–94)*

Luck doesn't come into it. The way you think does. Your attitude does.

Your success is your responsibility. It isn't anyone else's. When I first started my own business, getting an appointment with a prospective client was on a scale of difficulty somewhere between virtually impossible and 'forget it'. I had no track record, and most companies either believed training was a waste of time or had a preferred supplier with whom they were quite content. So when at last a prospective client asked me to make a formal proposal for a team-building programme, it was all I could do to stop myself from breaking into the Hallelujah Chorus. The only problem was that although I knew that my methodology could easily be incorporated into a team-building event, I had little experience of team-building, and I wasn't sure how an effective team-building course was constructed. Then a friend put me in contact with a former SAS instructor in Hereford.

It's hard to imagine anyone better qualified to give a lesson in team-building, and what I learned from him and his team was a revelation. At the core of SAS beliefs are perseverance, determination and personal responsibility. The instructors I met at Hereford told me that the recruits who fail the physically punishing selection course ultimately fail themselves, either because they haven't prepared, or more simply because they choose to quit. You only fail when you quit: that is the recurring theme in SAS philosophy. Those who pass selection, they said, suffer no less pain than all the rest: their lungs burn as much, their feet are as sore, their muscles as strained. The difference is that those who pass find deep within themselves the determination to take one more step. They don't blame others, or look to a generous instructor in the hope he'll turn a blind eye, or seek excuses for failure. They have prepared, they have committed, and they have taken responsibility for their own success.

**Some people make things happen, some watch things happen, and some wonder what happened.**
*Anon.*

I learned too that by the third day of the selection process, long before it gets serious, the instructors can pick out those who will later pass. What they are perceiving here can also be perceived in the broader context. We have all met people with a special something – charisma, leadership, powerful self-confidence – that marks them out as individuals bound for the top, people who attract others through their personality, who make everything seem effortless. These individuals have the feel of natural born winners, and we can pick them out as easily as the SAS instructors pick out those who will pass selection.

What they all have in common is a very clear idea of where they are going, a plan that will get them there, and an unshakable belief that they will arrive – strengths that we already have, but that most of us have forgotten how to access and to use. As life has shaped both our self-image and our attitude to the world, we have learned to hope for the best while expecting the worst. But we all started in life as natural born winners, and if we really want to, we can reconnect with the winner within.

## Chance or design?

Just as success is your responsibility and not a question of luck, so chance in itself plays almost no part in your path to success; what does play a part is the perception you have of chance and your readiness to convert it to your ends. For it is only when you focus on realising a goal that you will perceive chance events as opportunities.

**Luck is what happens when preparation meets opportunity.**
*Seneca the Elder (c. 55 BC–c. AD 39), Roman rhetorician and writer*

Let's take a simple case that we can all identify with. You decide that you would like a short holiday in a warm climate. What do you do first? You choose where you want to go and when. This is a clearly defined decision. Of course, you could just leave it to chance and jump in the car when the fancy takes you and without any idea of a destination, but then you might end up spending the whole day debating whether to turn right or left at the first crossroads.

So you've planned when and where you're going; now you plan how. You work out a route, you buy maps, devise back-up plans, budget costs. You may take a chance on finding accommodation when you get there, to give yourself added flexibility, but you'll probably research all the places within your budget. In effect, you leave little or nothing to chance before you go. And it's precisely because you've done all this careful planning that you're now able to be flexible in small ways. Here's an example. You're well on your way and feeling hungry when you come across an attractive roadside restaurant that you never knew existed. Now, simply because you're en route to a planned destination, you're able to take advantage of the opportunity the restaurant provides.

It is only when we have a clearly defined objective that we are able to take advantage of apparently random chances, because it is only then that we recognise the opportunity they offer. Put it another way. If you go through life looking for the lucky break without knowing exactly what you want to achieve in the long term, then it's an odds-on certainty that you won't be able to recognise opportunities when you come across them.

**Opportunities pass, they don't pause.**

*Anon.*

When I was eighteen, I hitchhiked by myself around Europe. During my six-week adventure I was often the recipient of much kindness. Once in Italy a driver who had been behaving very oddly suddenly stopped and ordered me out of the car. It was about 10 pm and I felt very alone as I stood by the side of the main autostrada to Milan. No one was likely to stop so I walked towards a light in the distance, and soon arrived in a small village where many people were sitting at long tables eating and drinking. I was immediately made welcome as food and drink was put in front of me. No one spoke any English and I spoke no Italian, but I do remember having a wonderful time. At the end of the evening a bed was found for me and the next morning I awoke to find a simple breakfast laid out. As I walked out of the village many locals from the previous evening bid me farewell. On another occasion I was ill and got a lift from a doctor who gave me a prescription for medicine. Throughout my trip I had many chance encounters – from which I was able to benefit. Where the chance encounters were threatening or, as one one occasion even dangerous, I was able to avoid trouble by immediately recognising the situation – and taking appropriate action. I had realised that experiences I had were in themselves neither simply 'good' nor 'bad'. What mattered was my ability to put each of them into the context of the whole trip. When opportunities arose I would seize them and use them to my advantage, and threats were avoided at all costs. Both types of response were a matter of personal perspective.

It's not chance itself that counts: it's what we make of it. We can have a good idea of the outcome of a given project before we start, but no guarantee. An American who had been through great trauma in his life, losing two businesses as a result of two near-fatal accidents which left him badly scarred and in a wheelchair, went on to create a third, successful, business. When asked the secret of his success, he said simply, 'It's not what's happened to you that matters, it's what you do about it.'

If the success you seek depends solely on luck, may I wish you good luck – because you'll be waiting around a long time.

## Self-image

**The you you see is the you you'll be.**

In his classic book of 1960, *Psycho-Cybernetics*, Maxwell Maltz describes his experiences as a Californian plastic surgeon treating people who wanted to improve their appearance. He tells the story of a beautiful woman intent on having a small blemish removed; she found it unsightly and consequently felt very unattractive. Realising that she was unlikely to listen to reason, he agreed to perform the procedure. He happened to notice, meanwhile, that the woman's boyfriend, a short, unattractive man, had an ugly mole on his face. But when he mentioned that he could correct it, the man looked confused and said, 'There's nothing wrong with my appearance.'

This man's powerful image of himself as attractive affected the way he acted, the way he conducted business and – crucially – the way he thought about himself. It made him who he was. His girlfriend was the opposite. In spite of her beauty she had no real confidence in her looks, and the blemish became so magnified in her mind that it reinforced her inner conviction that she was fundamentally unattractive.

The quality of our self-image – positive or negative – is central to our potential for success.

Take the example of a child learning to walk. On average, he will fall over about 240 times before succeeding. It's almost as if nature were saying to him, 'Don't quit, because when you quit you only fail.'

What happens is that the fallen child picks himself up and, using the feedback information learned and stored for ever in the brain, automatically adapts so as to correct his mental image of the walking process. His abilities to learn, to acquire and to achieve are inborn, and they are formidably powerful. However many falls the child takes, his self-image is unwaveringly that of being able to walk. He doesn't get disheartened; he doesn't think of himself as a failure when he meets a setback; he knows, unconsciously, that he is going to learn from his mistakes.

By adulthood, this innate conviction of inner potential has atrophied in most people. But the interesting thing here is that *successful* individuals and businesses always have a strong self-image; they too believe without any doubt at all that they can reach their goals. Such individuals accept that the process of falling over, of making mistakes, is part of the progress they are making towards their objective, and that it is in no way a reflection on who they are. This ability to accept that failure is not an expression of your being, but part of the process, is an essential ingredient of success.

A study in America showed that 96 per cent of four-year-olds had high self-esteem and a strong self-image. These children believed that the world was at their feet: they could become astronauts, ballerinas, doctors, cowboys, pilots – whatever they wanted. Their typical fantasy games showed how clearly they were able to visualise these dreams. The shocking part of the study was that by the time they reached eighteen less than 5 per cent had a good self-image. Along the way they had been told, 'You can't sing, You're clumsy, Hey, stupid! Who do you think you are? You'll never be a success.' As we grow older, our self-image is moulded increasingly by external influences, whether it be a teacher telling us we're incapable of learning, a parent insisting we're clumsy, or even a friend who, with the best intentions, implies repeatedly that our cooking is hopeless. Such comments are collected and stored in the subconscious mind; and our subconscious mind uses them to undermine our original self-image and replace it with a more doubting one.

The problem is that if you have a poor self-image, you will always be looking for evidence to reflect or confirm it. If you believe you can't cook and you find yourself in a situation where you have to, you know something is going to go wrong. The minute it does, your first response is, 'I've always known I can't cook' – perfectly in tune with your current self-image. As far as your subconscious is concerned, you are a person who can't cook – this is who you are – and you will always look for evidence to reinforce this idea of yourself.

> **If you think you can or think you can't, you're usually right.**
>
> *Henry Ford (1863–1947)*

How much, by contrast, is possible with a strong self-image? I remember asking the former SAS instructor in Hereford what he thought was the greatest thing the regiment had ever done. He offered me several alternatives: the Iranian Embassy rescue, their contribution in the Falklands War, the Gulf War. I disagreed with all of these. In my view, I told him, the greatest thing the regiment ever did was at its creation, to call itself the *Special* Air Service. Consequently, it thinks of itself as special and, more importantly, its enemies think of it as special too. This sense of specialness is further intensified by the rigours of the selection process, and the continual references by SAS instructors to the regiment's history, which reinforce the idea that its members are part of a unique elite. Given an image this strong at the core of its operations, it is easy to imagine the confidence instilled in every individual.

Equally, in the corporate world there are companies that have developed a powerful, winning image that stays intact even in the most adverse conditions. And when any company has this degree of self-belief, when it combines a strong sense of its past success, firm visionary leadership and confidence in all its activities, it creates the ability not just to set seemingly impossible targets but to achieve them.

In 1959 Honda set themselves the goal of being a major automotive player in America within thirty years. The suggestion seemed folly: American manufacturers had a virtual monopoly then on US car sales, and the few foreign manufacturers effectively competed only in the luxury market. Yet within the estimated time span, Honda had realised their goal.

When the California legislature decided to introduce a statute that would make a 50mpg low-emission engine a legal requirement for small cars, the response of the American car industry was to attempt to overturn the proposed legislation, to raise a war fund of millions of dollars and hire lobbyists in Washington to plead their case. Honda, on the other hand, responded differently. They simply rose to the challenge and, even though they had no real idea of how such a technological leap could be made, declared that they were going to make this engine. The story of how they did it is a masterclass in determination, creativity and focus. Their engineers beat the US deadline, creating the most technologically advanced engine currently in mass production, the Honda VTEC.

**They can because they believe they can.**
*Virgil (c. 70–19 B.C.) Roman poet*

## Destiny

The self-belief, the identification of a goal and the commitment and perseverance that lead to its realisation are sometimes spoken of in terms of 'destiny'. When people talk of destiny they frequently do so in quasi-mystical terms, implying a predestination in which the unfolding of the moment of success is ordained by unseen forces. Many successful figures of the twentieth century have also had a sense of destiny, though not one that was necessarily preordained.

When, as a twenty-two-year-old, my golfing hero Seve Ballesteros won the British Open in 1979, he said the win was his 'destiny'. Like virtually every great sportsman and woman who has reached the top, he had always had the absolute conviction that, come what might, he would one day get there.

What many call 'destiny' is, I believe, the result of a very clearly visualised goal that has become the driving force in an individual's pursuit of success. I can't prove it, but I doubt there is a single Wimbledon or FA Cup champion who has not from childhood seen himself one day standing at that point where he has ultimately arrived. I'm willing to concede that when people with a great natural talent win a particular event they may sometimes be justified in attributing their success to good fortune and to finding form on the day; but scratch deeper, and you will find someone who has dreamt big and unconsciously put into place the seeds of their own success. They might call it 'fate' or 'destiny', but I think George Bernard Shaw knew better. 'People are always blaming their circumstances for what they are,' he wrote. 'I don't believe in circumstances. The people who get on in this world are the people who get up and look for the circumstances they want, and, if they can't find them, make them.' These people determined to make things happen. I do not believe the future exists in an inescapable form. It is our actions here and now that determine our future experiences.

Our destinies are for the most part determined by the goals we set. Do you dream big, and hope it will happen? Or have you stopped dreaming so as to avoid disappointment?

**Whatever you can do, or dream you can do, begin it. Boldness has genius, power and magic in it.**
*Johann Wolfgang von Goethe (1749–1832),*
*German poet, dramatist, novelist and scientist*

When something goes wrong, so many people express their disappointment in comments such as 'I knew that was going to happen.' And they'll speak with the same conviction of being *generally* unlucky, or clumsy, or unsuccessful – 'Why does it always happen to me?' The heart of their argument is that events in their lives demonstrate time and time again that they are simply unlucky, have always been unlucky, and expect to remain so. But the reality is that they have created a powerful belief in their own misfortune, and anything that happens to them serves to reinforce that belief. They store the experience in their subconscious mind, thus confirming their poor self-image. When, on the other hand, they enjoy good fortune, they experience it as so much at odds with the 'unsuccessful' person they believe themselves to be that they simply dismiss it, thereby avoiding any conflict of self-image.

> **To be wronged is nothing unless you continue to remember it.**
> *Confucius (c. 551–479 BC), Chinese sage*

I remember talking with an extremely successful business figure who insisted that he was very clumsy, that as a child he was always banging into tables, dropping things, spilling drinks. He was, I suspect, not very different in his childhood development from you or me, the only difference probably being that every time he dropped something, or knocked something over, his parents told him he was a clumsy boy. And yet this man at the same time told me proudly of his accomplishments as a pilot and a rock-climber – both of which, it goes without saying, require a high degree of concentration and coordination. It was only when the discrepancy was pointed out to him – that in leisure activities he was so accomplished while in social situations he still considered himself clumsy – that he was at last able to begin to let go of that awkward label that had been hanging around his neck for so many years.

If you consciously or unconsciously think of yourself as clumsy, unsuccessful, ugly, unmusical – or whatever it is that you hold at the core of your self-image in your subconscious mind – that same subconscious will sabotage or deliberately filter away from you any information that might contradict, or conflict with, your self-image. And it's the quality of that self-image that will determine how you will deal with the obstacles on your path to success.

## Setbacks

Individuals and businesses alike inevitably suffer setbacks of one kind and another. But if we have a clear belief in, and a commitment to continuing towards, the realisation of our goal, often through adversity, if we are able to create a 'never-quit' personal philosophy, then we will see setbacks simply as obstacles to overcome, as challenges to our ingenuity. If we don't have these strengths, on the other hand, setbacks will be the tools that destroy our self-belief. They will become insurmountable problems and wreck our confidence in our ability to complete the task we have undertaken.

The individual or company that has a negative attitude will identify even minor setbacks as major problems to be grappled with. This view of things, often combined with a lack of clearly defined goals, generally leads to a great deal of time and energy being spent fire-fighting, or knee-jerking to every event or situation perceived to be outside the norm.

The story of Honda and the Californian legislation for a new fuel-efficient engine is a good case in point. Rather than seeing the legislation as a major setback, Honda took it as an opportunity, convinced that they could make it work even though they didn't yet know how. The American car manufacturers by contrast saw it as yet another business-damaging initiative, and rather than try to solve the problem they set out to have the legislation removed. Two distinctly different approaches to the same problem: one visionary and ultimately successful, the other weak and embattled.

**Opportunity is missed by most people because it is dressed in overalls and looks like work.**
*Thomas Edison (1847–1931), American inventor*

Successful people put setbacks in perspective. They recognise that things that are beyond their control – to do with bank interest rates, the weather, the reliability of associates, will often go wrong, for example. What they do is accept it, accommodate it, and move on with the task in hand.

Too many of us use setbacks as an excuse for having failed to achieve what we set out to do: 'My partner ran off with the money', 'The bank called in the loan', 'Our major supplier went bust'. There is never a shortage of such setbacks, which, for one reason or another, made us give up. But actually, what we've done is quit. What we didn't have, to use a boxing analogy, is the ability to take a standing count, clear our heads, refocus and get on with the task we set out to achieve.

Whatever the circumstances.

## Commitment

Riding through setbacks towards your goal requires more than just a strong self-belief and a clearly defined objective. It takes commitment. Commitment is similar to determination, except that whereas determination may be an emotion of the moment, commitment is a steely underlying will that endures through all changes in circumstance. A massive factor in success, it is an intangible ingredient to which much lip-service is paid, and, dangerously, a quality which within a work situation is especially easy to fake.

Think about it. At work a new initiative is implemented or a training programme put in place. The management asks, requests politely, or perhaps demands that the staff make a commitment to seeing the policy through. Of course, officially everyone is on board. Everyone says they're committed. But are they?

We have all at some time in our lives, with the noblest of intentions, determined to change that ever-present aspect of our lives that we feel can always be improved on: our weight and/or our fitness. We buy a book, we join a gym, do whatever we feel is required to get us started. And we all know, I guess, what usually happens next.

> **Good thoughts are no better than good dreams if you don't follow through.**
> *Ralph Waldo Emerson (1803–82), American essayist*
> *and poet*

There won't be any problems this time. It's really going to work, it's going to be different from all the other times. You are determined, you've splashed out on a fancy machine called the calorie-counter-o-matic and bought enough fresh fruit and vegetables to worry an environmentalist. You've even joined a gym and invested in an ergonomically approved pair of branded sweat-pants. You are *very* committed.

You get up early and prepare your bowl of bran and oatmeal with relish, follow with half a grapefruit and wash it down with a cup of rosehip tea. Later, at the gym, you go through the prescribed exercises and return home feeling very pleased with yourself. But as the days go by, the results are slow to materialise and you start to feel your enthusiasm waning. Only slightly, at the beginning, but as the weeks pass your commitment all but disappears until finally you really can't be bothered any more and so the diet or fitness regime joins the list of previous failed attempts. And with each failed attempt you know deep down that the likelihood of a future attempt failing has increased.

Ultimately we fail on these occasions because, no matter how much we may protest at the notion, we *expected* to fail. What we took for real commitment was no more than desire. Someone once said that gratitude is the shortest-lived emotion. Perhaps – but I believe enthusiasm comes a close second. Enthusiasm, which in team events can generate so much energy and excitement, is in the last analysis no substitute for commitment. Imagine you've been in an accident and arrive at the hospital to find two doctors waiting on stand-by, one very enthusiastic, the other very committed – which one would you like to treat you?

When you commit to an objective, you have to do so with one hundred per cent belief that you are going to realise it. The commitment switch has two positions: on and off. There is no in between – you can no more be slightly committed than you can be slightly pregnant. And it is the passionate commitment in the minds of successful achievers that stops them ever quitting, that keeps them believing and persevering no matter how hard the going gets, because they know that in the end they're going to get there.

Examine the depth of your commitment to something or someone you absolutely believe in – your family, a loved one – and imagine what you would be prepared to do to help them in time of adversity. It's a powerful feeling. And it's the level of feeling you need to create in the process of making yourself truly committed to success.

> **Your life is up to you. Life provides the canvas;**
> **you do the painting.**
>
> *Anon.*

## Courage

Along with real commitment, success requires courage. We often associate courage with bravery, and though I have no doubt they are closely related, bravery has perhaps more to do with extraordinary, even impulse-driven, personal responses to exceptional situations where life itself may be at stake. Our own capacity for bravery is something that may never in our lives be tested. Courage, on the other hand, is a quality that we all possess and need to use daily; and when we do so, we start to make remarkable progress.

Courage is the ability to do something that, for whatever reason, we instinctively fear. It can be something we experience every day – fear of ridicule, fear of failure, fear of change – or a host of other things from which we naturally draw back. And we draw back because then we feel safe, and although what we thereby achieve is not what we would ideally have wished, it is at least something we are comfortable and familiar with.

But when we remain with the familiar, change becomes harder and harder; we become more risk-averse, and we reinforce the barriers that make us content to leave things just the way they are. Success only begins to happen when individuals with self-belief and the passion to succeed are prepared to pass through their fears and learn from the experience.

**Only those who dare to fail greatly can ever achieve greatly.**
*Robert F. Kennedy (1925–68)*

It's rather like someone on the flying trapeze who won't let go, won't make that essential first move in the acrobatic feat he's about to perform, because as long as he hangs on he is safe. Eventually he gets tired and runs out of momentum, and ends up dangling, going nowhere. In time, he gives up, falls and lands in the safety-net. By contrast, the artist who becomes a star is the one who, though afraid to let go, believes it can be done because the worst that can happen is that she'll land in the safety-net and learn from her mistake. Similarly, in order to get to where we want to go, we often need to find the courage to let go of where we are, by facing our fears and learning from our mistakes. The fuel that fires our courage – to start up in business, to explore an unmapped land, or simply to learn a new skill – is the passionate belief that success is not only achievable, but guaranteed.

For success-oriented people it is not the fear of failure that holds them back, but the fear of living their lives less fully and regretting the things they never attempted.

At the end of our lives we don't regret the things at which we failed; we regret the things we wished for and never attempted.

Let's suppose you're starting your own business. You get a fax line installed in your bedroom, have stationery printed, and flyers distributed locally, and send a hundred letters to prospective clients. Nothing happens. So you decide the next step is to set up meetings: the dreaded cold call. The problem is that, try as you might, you can't do it – you just want to quit every time you're halfway through dialling the number. Even if you do get through its odds on you'll be so nervous that you'll ramble on pointlessly, apologise for calling, and fail to secure a meeting. Why? Because the fear of rejection, of being patronised, typically causes us to pull back from a commitment to trying. Our imagined sense of failure is greater than our imagined sense of success. Strangely, the courage we require to overcome this is not so different from the courage of our personal heroes. It demands perseverance and the setting of achievable objectives; entertaining no doubts in their future success; focusing clearly on those objectives; and committing ourselves to not quitting under any circumstances.

When it comes to the much feared cold call, commit yourself to making five every day, then twenty, then forty, until you *deconstruct* the limiting belief that you have created. You will then perceive the cold call as part of the process, without which that process will not function.

The main fear that has to be overcome in life is fear of

failure itself. Failure is something that happens, a lesson to be learned from: it is not evidence that you are a failure bound always to fail. Jack Nicklaus, the greatest golfer of the modern era, told one young professional embarking on his career that he never forgot that he had failed a lot more frequently than he had succeeded.

We must learn to see failure as part of the learning curve: when we fail, it just means that we are not doing it – whatever it may be – right. Surveys of the most successful salespeople in America, those who are consistently the highest performers, have shown that the one thing they all have in common is that they started to get appointments and sell their products only after the sixth or seventh approach. These salespeople were not lucky; they were committed and courageous enough to have overcome the fear of rejection.

How do you find that courage? The answer is simple. Focus so clearly on your objective that you see and understand every step in the direction of its completion as an essential part of the process.

> **Do the thing you fear, and the death of fear is certain.**
>
> *Ralph Waldo Emerson*

## Belief

I mentioned earlier in this chapter the importance of self-image. The image you have of yourself is the person that people meet. We are all too aware when someone is being a 'phoney' – all the image-consulting and window-dressing in the world will be unable to disguise a poor self-image for long.

Your beliefs at both a corporate and – most importantly – a personal level represent your core values. They dictate how you approach problems, respond to situations, conduct all aspects of your behaviour.

These core values are rather like the DNA in your body: no matter from which part of you you take the sample, the information contained within it is exactly the same. And it's this information that provides the blueprint for your physical make-up. Similarly, your core values have a consistency that informs every aspect of your behaviour. So if you believe absolutely that you will succeed, almost anything becomes possible. A strong belief system can enable individuals to achieve seemingly impossible aims, allowing them to overcome fear, ridicule, hardship and even pain; a strong belief system can enable them to dissociate themselves at a personal level from difficulties or setbacks.

But a strong belief system is not about vague life-goals such as 'I hope to start my own business but I'm not sure what it'll be . . .' or 'I hope, if I'm lucky, to get a pay rise . . .' or 'I'm waiting to see what happens . . .'

**If your train's on the wrong track, every station you come to is the wrong station.**
*Bernard Malamud (1914–86), American novelist*

Our true beliefs are not about wish-fulfilment, but about believing that the goal we have set out to realise already exists in the future. Believe with one hundred per cent certainty that success is achievable and that failures along the way are no more than life offering you a learning experience, and you will create an inner confidence that needs no image-consulting or window-dressing. The you that people meet is a person with a very clear idea of where he or she is going in life. Your core beliefs are not only the foundation of your actions – they permeate your thinking. And how you think impacts directly on how you act, behave and live your life.

**Two men look through prison bars; one sees mud, the other stars.**
*Frederick Langbridge (1849–1923)*

# Fear

However strong our commitment, courage and belief, it will always help us to understand our fear. Fear in itself is not a bad thing: it can draw our attention to a future challenge and serve as a wake-up call to the fact that action needs to be taken. The fear response is a basic instinct that keeps us alert to serious danger; but in our daily encounters there are less dangerous situations to which we react with variations on the theme of fear – feelings that range from a general uneasiness, through anxiety, panic and paralysing stress. Our bodies physically manifest the emotional response to being afraid; fear causes our hearts to race, palms to sweat and stomachs to get butterflies. It is these emotional responses to our fear that hold us back.

In business, fear of failure and fear of change are the two factors that most hinder progress. It is interesting to note how many businesses have had to fail – often spectacularly – before, driven by the basic need to survive, they have made the very changes they previously felt unable to make.

I believe that most fears are based on events that have happened nowhere other than in our imagination. It has been said that fear is a dark-room where negatives are developed, and that it's an acronym for False Expectations Appearing Real; but whatever spin you put on it, the things we tend to fear are not those that have happened or are happening, but those that we believe might well. We will examine this in more detail later. But think for a moment now about the time and energy you put into creating fear-inducing negative scenarios, and then imagine how different it would be if that same time and energy were spent thinking about successful outcomes.

**The happiness of your life depends upon the quality of your thoughts.**
*Marcus Antonius (AD 86–161)*

There is a story of a prisoner in a Chinese gaol in the 1930s who, a week after his trial, had been sentenced to death. His guards kept a close eye on him, to stop him depriving them of his public execution. But whenever they visited his cell they were amazed to find him cheerful, writing letters, singing, and ready to joke with them. They thought he was crazy, and as the days passed his behaviour never varied. On the day of his execution, the guards brought him his last meal. One, unable to bear it any longer, asked the prisoner how he could be so cheerful, knowing he was so soon to die. He answered, 'I am alive now. The future, for all its certainties, has yet to reveal itself, so now I'll enjoy being alive.'

Ask yourself, then, what you are afraid of and why. I'm not taking about phobias, which often have their roots in childhood traumas, though these too when faced can be overcome. I'm talking about those 'events' in the future that you believe are going to happen. The fact is that the more you vividly believe them to be inevitable the more strongly they are forming in your mind as *real* future events. And more often than not, once you believe it strongly enough, happen they will.

When it comes to business, I know that for many companies the risk that a wrong decision may bring with it is bankruptcy. However, it is my experience that by the time the risks inherent in a given decision are threatening to materialise, the roots of the problem have been there for months, if not years, before. Yet, as fear has more and more paralysed them into inaction, rather than facing the challenge courageously the management has arranged loans and called in consultants and general soothsayers.

Fear traps us in our past: it is extraordinary how often with friends and colleagues we enjoy reminiscing about 'the good old days', when everything was more secure. Of course it was: the past is always more secure – it can't change. And when we do think back, we tend in any case to select happy experiences. But we don't seem to laugh and joke so much about the future and what it may hold, or speculate on why we delay making positive changes in our personal and professional lives. Perhaps it's because we're adhering to the procrastinator's motto, 'Next year I'll get it done' – and in the meantime we'll stay where we are, because compared with what we imagine awaits us, the past is a pretty safe place to be.

Remember that no matter how real whatever it is you fear will happen in the future appears to be, it has not *in fact* happened. Recognise the illusory nature of the fear, and let it go. Imagine a successful outcome and replace it with that; and focus all your efforts on making that new future a reality.

## Motivation

One night after the late shift, a man decided to take a short cut home by way of the cemetery. It was raining hard and the wind was blowing, and suddenly in the dark of the night he fell into a freshly dug grave. He landed heavily, and now he was wet, covered in mud and angry at his misfortune. However, he was fit and very determined to get out, so he tried to jump; then when that proved useless he took a run up – but again without luck, so now he thought he'd try climbing. The soil was clay-based, though, and he couldn't get a hold, so finally he decided to curl up into a ball in a corner, try and stay warm, and call for help in the morning. He settled down accordingly, and drifted off to sleep.

As it happened, some twenty minutes later another fellow from the same shift, also taking a short cut through the cemetery, stumbled into the same freshly dug grave. Now this fellow had had a few drinks, and was little and rather unfit. All the same, he tried first to jump out, then to climb – but without success; for a full fifteen minutes he put all his effort into escaping his current predicament, but to no avail. Exhausted, he was standing there in the dark and the rain when suddenly from the corner of the grave he heard a voice 'You'll never get out of here,' it said ominously.

But he did. As soon as he heard the voice he jumped straight up and out.

Our motivation is an internal action, which we control, though frequently it is external experiences which act as the trigger to finally push us into action. When a company talks about its motivated staff, you can be sure it has created powerful motivators to get those people to act. Motivators are powerful catalysts inspiring us into action: whether basic ones like hunger or dramatic ones like the voice from the grave, they fuel our dreams. Apart from hunger, at the basic level our motivators are survival and shelter. Our hunger motivates us to find food, our need for warmth motivates us to find shelter, and so on. In the sporting world there have been coaching legends who have understood the powerful force of a motivated team; these individuals have known that passion and commitment are internal experiences for each individual player – experiences which, unlike interest or attention, cannot be faked. But passion and commitment are like oxygen and petrol in the combustion engine – they require the external spark of motivation to create power.

Successful organisations often create or identify motivators for their staff, basing those motivators sometimes on fear (loss of job, demotion etc.), sometimes on receptiveness to praise (talk of promotion, expressions of appreciation, promise of financial reward). In other businesses, the sort that tick over uneventfully year after year, a general complacency within senior management and the lack of a clear vision of the organisation's future prevent the business from growing: they seem quite happy to play catch-up with their competitors. Then one dark day they discover that they are being eyed up for a hostile take-over. Suddenly, it's this external factor that motivates the company: firstly into forming cohesive teams; secondly into focusing on a definite strategy; and finally, the desperate nature of the situation forces them to make concrete decisions.

Companies that are in rapid growth continually keep themselves motivated by never allowing themselves to be lulled into a false sense of security. They are continually setting themselves new goals. They are motivated to be successful in clearly defined terms within a well-thought-out and strategised business plan; they are so passionate about what they do that their desire for success in itself becomes a motivator.

But you can no more motivate yourself by saying, 'I've got to get motivated' than you can get fit by simply joining a gym and waiting for something to happen. You have to identify the triggers in your life, then go out there and use them and make them work for you, just like the machines in the gym.

At one conference I spoke at, a young fellow came up to me and asked me how I could motivate *him*. I told him that, short of pulling a gun on him, I didn't have a clue. The purpose of my talk, I explained, had been to share with the audience my experiences and thoughts, and in the process to inform, amuse and hopefully inspire them to act and to believe in their ability to make real changes. I hoped the talk would spark them into action. The commitment and passion must come from within – and that, I said, was *his* responsibility.

# 2    Your Brain

> **It is not enough to have a good mind; the main thing is to use it well.**
> *René Descartes (1596–1650), French philosopher*

All achievements, from the grandest to the most humble, began life in one person's imagination as an idea. We think and dream in images, and those dreams and images exist only in our minds, so it's worth taking a look at the old grey matter. Actually, the brain is more of a beige colour, so to be technically correct I suppose we should call it 'the old beige matter'.

Much has been written about the brain, and yet it is still the least understood part of the body. Experts tell us that we utilise only 5 per cent of its potential, and that the brain is more powerful than the world's mightiest computer. The most important thing to understand about the brain is that how we think dictates everything we do, and though genetic inheritance may account for 50 per cent of our mental process, that still leaves 50 per cent that we can develop and control.

And consider just how much the brain is capable of. Think of John Milton in his old age memorising *Paradise Lost*, or of Mozart having composed, by the age of thirteen, concertos, sonatas, symphonies, an operetta and an opera. We have all heard of people with extraordinary mental abilities in mathematics and in memory, but the interesting thing is that such abilities don't necessary conform to conventional models of intelligence. Take the condition known as autism, for many years one of medicine's mysteries. People suffering from autism are classified as socially dysfunctional and have serious learning difficulties, yet some of them are capable of the most extraordinary feats of memory, and have outstanding mathematical and musical abilities.

So let's be clear – your brain is not just the most complex organ in your body, it's the single most evolved organ in the world. It is living matter, it has the capacity to regenerate itself, and every memory that it stores it can recall for future use, for the whole of your life. It never switches off; it never stops working; it is the source of all our experience, our hopes, our beliefs, our intuition – ourselves. And, as the brain is the home of all our thoughts, our dreams and ambitions, the better we are able to understand and develop the thinking process, the more rapidly we shall increase our efficiency and progress towards our goals.

When compared with all the earlier research, advances since the 1960s in explaining the brain's complex neurophysiology have been phenomenal, but the more we discover the more we realise we are still just scratching the surface.

Nonetheless, there are some fundamental insights we can gain into the structure, and function, and the thinking processes of the brain, that will put into perspective the Natural Born Winner techniques of mentally conditioning one's approach to success. I've always thought the brain is nature's greatest creation – unfortunately it came without an instruction manual, and the sooner we harness its potential, the better.

## Its structure

Detailed analysis of the structure of the brain – unless you are studying to be a neurosurgeon – is rather boring which is due in no small part to its being this very complex organ full of unpronounceable Latin names, as I discovered when studying human biology at university. I

# Robin's simple guide to the brain

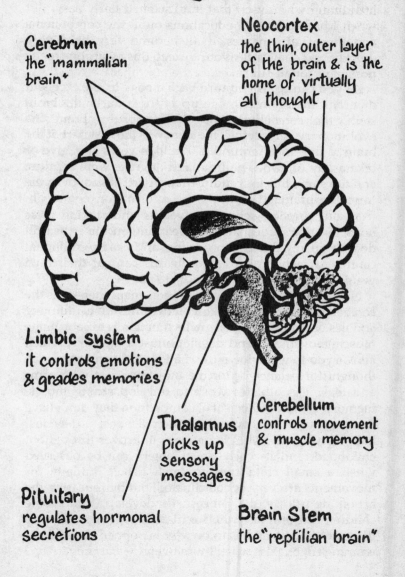

**Cerebrum**
the "mammalian brain"

**Neocortex**
the thin, outer layer of the brain & is the home of virtually all thought

**Limbic system**
it controls emotions & grades memories

**Thalamus**
picks up sensory messages

**Cerebellum**
controls movement & muscle memory

**Pituitary**
regulates hormonal secretions

**Brain Stem**
the "reptilian brain"

remember having to dissect a brain and, while a friend was being told off by the tutor for doing a rather lamentable impersonation of Dr Frankenstein, thinking a little smugly to myself that it all seemed fairly easy. But when I had to learn the locations of all the components and those Latin names, it all became very hard very quickly. So I shall endeavour to keep this as jargon-free as possible – for all our sakes.

As you can see if you turn back a page to my excellent diagram, the brain is made up of three parts: the brain stem, the cerebellum and the cerebrum. From the evolutionary perspective, the stem was the first part of the brain to develop – around 270 million years ago, give or take a day or two. The first land animals were reptiles, and the stem, this first rudimentary part, is known as the 'reptilian brain'. It controls the information coming in from our physical senses, as well as undertaking basic housekeeping duties such as breathing and heartbeat. It doesn't do any thinking or feeling, and has no emotional centre – which explains why lizards can eat their own young, and don't make affectionate pets.

Next to evolve – about forty million years later – was the cerebellum, which looks like a bit of rather old cauliflower and lies behind the brainstem. Its function is to coordinate muscle movements and develop muscle memory, which allows you to walk down the road without any conscious thought for balance or for the movements of your arms and legs. Top athletes work to develop strong muscle memory, so that in the heat of competition they don't have to concentrate on controlling their actions – they just happen naturally. Muscle memory improves throughout childhood, and its early development can be observed when a small child tries to catch a ball. Initially his movements are very uncoordinated, but by repeating the action he allows the process to develop, with some children learning faster and achieving higher skill levels than others. (Which has to be why I dropped that match-winning rugby pass when I was twelve – *must* be.)

The third part – about 160 million years old – is the cerebrum, and this is where as a student I started getting confused. It is also known as the 'mammalian brain' (which explains why dogs are affectionate and *don't* eat their young) and is the location of our thinking and emotions. The particular features of the cerebrum as it has developed in *Homo sapiens* constitute a vital part of what distinguishes us as human beings, and the rest of this chapter will try to help you avoid its complexity while fully appreciating its extraordinary potential.

In the early days of brain research, scientists thought that the different parts of the cerebrum held different information – one area stored knowledge on geography, for instance, another on friends' birthdays, and so on. It is now accepted, however, that each memory and thought links up different areas of the brain, and this aspect of brain function is called 'multiple mapping'. Multiple mapping is very important, for two reasons. First, because the whole brain is used in the thinking process and in the creation of memory, it is important in its role of keeping the brain's internal lines of communication (the neuro-transmitters) healthy and functioning – this is just as important as keeping your arteries unblocked. Second, the fact that memories are stored in different locations within the brain means that it is almost impossible completely to 'destroy' a memory.

Which is good to know. But of course the brain doesn't just control thoughts and memories. It is responsible for how we feel, too.

## A quick guided tour of your emotional centre

The limbic system began to evolve about 150 million years ago, and its development marked the creation of social cooperation within animal species. The system is made up of five parts, which collectively act as a kind of switchboard between the mind and the body. As we've already noted, the development of a winning approach to the future, how you think and feel about yourself is initially at least as important as what you do. So bear with me while I run through another bit of the somewhat dry subject of brain structure – it will give you an idea of why it is that how we think impacts directly on our self-image and behaviour.

First stop the hippocampus, the brain's memory centre. This is a temporary repository for short-term memories, and a few longer ones, but it ships most of our short-term memories out to a location in our neocortex (where, of course, they become long-term memories). The hippocampus operates largely as the place where we hold 'unemotional' facts – information such as school subjects with which we have no emotional association. It doesn't fully develop until a person is two years old, and researchers believe that this explains why we have no memories of early infancy. Interestingly, the hippocampus is the first area of damage when an individual develops Alzheimer's, a disease that causes the loss of short-term, but not long-term, memories. (Long-term memories are protected because they are already stored in the neocortex.)

Next, the amygdala, which processes emotional memories. It works with the thinking brain to decide how much emotional impact each memory will carry – your first day at school, your first kiss, the news of a national tragedy. If (and I certainly wouldn't recommend this) you were to have your amygdala surgically removed, you would be totally without emotional response, just like the lizard mentioned earlier. But, of course, this wouldn't bother you because you would be incapable of having any feeling about it.

Closely connected to the amygdala is the hypothalamus which, by relaying any given message to the pituitary gland, triggers the release of hormones, helping to tell the body how to respond to different situations. For example, when you find yourself in a situation that frightens you, adrenaline is released into your bloodstream, producing the 'fight or flight' response.

Next is the thalamus, part of whose job is to make sense of the constant flow of messages coming from your sensory organs (apart from that of smell); and finally your pituitary, a pea-sized object that through hormonal control tells the other glands in your hormonal system what to do.

Now, I would be the first to admit that this is a very simplified explanation of brain structure and emotional function, but when we come to apply it to mental conditioning and performance function you will see that it helps to complete the picture. It's important to realise that every experience creates a memory with an emotional association, so if, for instance, your emotional memories of failure are strong, when you face a new challenge memories will be recalled with their associated physical feelings. In fact, all future challenges will trigger a similar emotional sensation, so what we need to do is to find techniques for changing this negative pattern of response, and replace it with powerful positive images of future success.

## Conscious thought

Conscious thought is the state of mental awareness in the here and now. The reading of this book is a conscious act. You are fully aware of it, and you completely control it. Conscious thought is about awareness and choice. And it is the ability to weigh up information and make decisions using stored memories and present experience that makes us a unique species.

All the same the conscious mind, for all its extra-ordinary power, is effectively capable of only one thought at a time, just like a radio can be tuned in to only one station at a time. For example, have you ever had a conversation with someone while simultaneously trying to eavesdrop on another? It's virtually impossible. Or imagine trying to juggle three balls by consciously attempting to control each individual ball. It cannot be done, because your conscious mind cannot process that amount of information simultaneously.

But although, in order to avoid being overwhelmed by a flood of sensory data, we can be aware of only one thought at a time, the conscious mind gives us full control of our actions. In consequence, we have the power consciously to determine how we feel and respond to given situations. Let me give you an example. You are waiting for a bus when a car drives through a puddle close to where you are standing, dumping water on your shoes. In a physical reflex action, you jump back. Thereafter your response is a conscious one – in other words, you allow yourself to get frustrated, angry, whatever. On the other hand, if you wanted to, you could equally choose to see the soaking as a random act of chance, wish you didn't have wet feet and determine not to let it spoil your day or upset your equanimity. The point is that you consciously choose your response to a given situation, but that choice is often only the result of habit. And what your conscious mind can do is change your habits – if you choose.

> God grant me the serenity to accept the things I cannot change, the courage to change the things I can, and the wisdom to know the difference.
> *Reinhold Niebuhr (1892–1971), American Protestant theologian; 'The Serenity Prayer'*

Think of your conscious mind as like a computer screen; it can only process one image on its display, whilst simultaneously running many programmes. Our conscious minds control what we think about and how we think about it.

This ability consciously to control our thought process

is an essential ingredient in the creation of success. If you begin to focus on the positive, to put setbacks in perspective and not dwell on failure, you will begin to act in accordance with a healthy and positive self-image. You and you alone have the ability, if you so choose, to change the way you perceive yourself, and your career. Your conscious mind is your greatest asset when it comes to helping you change patterns of behaviour and how you feel about yourself, and will help you to program your subconscious mind to create future success.

> **Thought is the strongest thing we have. Work done by true and profound thought – that is a real force.**
> *Albert Schweitzer (1875–1965), theologian and medical missionary*

The fact that what you think is what you create is of critical importance in achieving success. Winners in whatever field do *not* dwell on the negative, or focus on failure; they consciously avoid these pitfalls. Because if you don't control the way you think, the way you think will continue to control *you*: you will repeat the mistakes and patterns of the past, and perpetuate or even create the very future you wish to escape from. So the first lesson is that it's up to you – and you can do it.

## The subconscious

Your subconscious mind collects and collates all the experiences that the senses pick up throughout your life, and stores them for future use. You know those golden Eureka! moments when the solution to a problem, or a brilliant creative insight, just comes to you? Or you suddenly remember an old schoolteacher's name, or pick up a crossword puzzle that stumped you an hour ago only to discover that you can now solve the remaining clues? These are perfect examples of the subconscious doing what it does best. Once your conscious mind had given it the problem, it never stopped working on the crossword puzzle or trying to locate the teacher's name among your long-term memories until it came up with what it was searching for.

Take a simple example of the subconscious mind at work. Have you ever walked into a store when shopping for a pair of shoes, and found that from the hundreds of pairs on display one suddenly jumps out at you (I don't mean literally)? Why is this? The explanation is that your subconscious mind scanned all the shoes, compared them with its stored information about your preferences, memories and associations, then, having sent the message to your conscious mind, in a split second automatically drew your attention to a particular pair.

If you had to explain why your eye initially fell on that particular pair, you might well talk of a 'feeling' that you find hard to articulate. It's certainly not a decision – that's for conscious thought. However, when the assistant starts showing you other, similar, pairs, you may now start consciously overriding the choice you made intuitively. And what you'll certainly find is that any conscious decision you make about the shoes will be much less rapid than the subconscious one. Why? Because unlike the subconscious mind, the conscious mind can only do one thing at a time.

When we read of the brain being able to carry out millions of actions simultaneously, we tend to think, 'Impossible!', but this is because we are able to be aware of only one thing at a time. Consider how, at a basic level, the brain manages our bodies – usually in ways of which we're quite unconscious. Every function of the body is being regulated, all the time; every one of the millions of receptors around the body – to do with heat, pain, pressure, balance, or whatever – is constantly passing feedback to the brain, giving it a continuous twenty-four hour status report. Depending on the information the brain receives, it instructs the body to respond accordingly. For instance, when we get too hot the brain responds by telling the body to begin sweating. Try right now consciously to make yourself sweat – impossible (unless you're a fakir). I know I can't do it. Yet the brain has evolved to do this automatically, along with a million other functions, and is still operating at only 5 per cent of its potential capacity! And, as hypnosis demonstrates, the subconscious mind can be programmed to reduce your heart rate, lower your temperature and even anaesthetise parts of your body. These extraordinary abilities, the result of actively conditioning the subconscious mind, highlight – if only at a physical level – the incredible potential we all have inside us to achieve anything we set our minds to.

In September 1985 I awoke one morning in a most unusual position, a position I'd never before and have never since woken up in. I was lying on my front with my left forearm across the back of my head, the fingers of my left hand resting very lightly on the right-hand side of my neck four inches below my ear. It was not a particularly comfortable position, but before I was aware of any discomfort, I felt under my fingers the presence of a hard pea-sized lump in my neck. Over the next twenty seconds I felt it from different angles and wondered why I had not noticed it before. When I went into the bathroom and looked in the mirror I could see no evidence of it; however, when I tilted my head to the left a very small lump protruded from below the skin.

I am not, and never have been, a hypochondriac, but I knew that this lump was bad news. In fact, I believed with absolute certainty that it was cancerous, and my first thought was that it was Hodgkin's disease (a cancer of the lymphatic system), as a close friend of mine had died of it three months previously. I went to see my GP, who told me it was a lump of hard fat. Later I asked three friends – all doctors, including my brother-in-law – to examine the lump: given that I had no other obvious symptoms, they all deduced that it was an old inflamed lymph node of which I had not previously been aware. By this time I did have one symptom – extreme fatigue – and then a blood test revealed a raised ESR (erythrocyte sedimentation rate) which is a non-specific test, but it indicated that there was something amiss. So my sister, who is a theatre sister, arranged for me to see a consultant surgeon at the Christie Hospital in Manchester.

The surgeon examined me, and said that it was impossible to tell what any lump was and that the only way to find out was to remove it. So a week later I went into the hospital and had the lump taken out. I returned to London, where I had to wait five days for the results. On the day before I was due to travel back to Manchester I actually stopped being anxious and felt for the first time that maybe I had just been imagining the whole episode; the blood test result could have a hundred possible causes, the exhaustion could be due to working long hours.

That evening I went to my sister's home for supper – it was her husband who had done the original blood test. Going into the kitchen at one point, I found him on the phone, grim-faced, my sister standing beside him. 'I think he should be told', I heard him say, and then he saw me. Turning towards me he said, 'The results have come through.' I remember looking at him and saying, 'They're not good.' 'No,' he replied. 'You've got Hodgkin's.'

Why had I woken up in that position all those weeks ago, and noticed a lump that would have taken six or eight more weeks to become obvious? Why had I con-tinued to seek medical opinions until my family, frustrated at my persistence, decided to get the matter sorted out once and for all? Why did I feel from the first moment that I had Hodgkin's? Surely not because a friend had just died of it. The incidence of Hodgkin's is one in thirty-five thousand, so it was clear that the chances of two friends having it were astronomically remote.

I believed then – and I understand now – that my subconscious was fully aware that something was not functioning as it should. I believe it drew my attention to the nature of my illness, it made me listen to the quiet voice within that we call intuition. I was fortunate to have medical friends and family: even then, it was my conviction that had made me persist after the numerous 'don't worries'. I knew I was not naturally a worrier about health matters, so I paid full attention to my feelings.

Though this experience gave me a greater appreciation of the value of listening to my body, in the operations and treatments that followed I never intuitively felt there was a point when I could say that the cancer was gone or that I was cured. I now believe I was consciously trying too hard to be aware of how I was feeling, focusing on the negatives, and remaining in too much of a daze to allow my subconscious to land its messages of good health in my conscious.

Paying attention to what the subconscious tells us is of enormous importance in every sphere of life – from choosing shoes to overcoming illness. By extension, I understand now that it is our most powerful ally in helping us as individuals to become winners. When I was first exposed to such ideas, I dismissed them as fanciful. I know now, and from direct experience, that they are the key component of successful living.

## What a computer!

Though the human brain is frequently compared with a computer, this undoubtedly oversimplifies the phenomenal sophistication of the brain and exalts the versatility of the computer. It's not just that the brain is capable of vastly more fact storage and memory access, than the world's most powerful computer. What I think is more remarkable is that, as I've already mentioned, we use only 5 per cent of our brain – or, more accurately, we use all of our brain but only to 5 per cent of its capacity. To put it in perspective, the brain has one hundred billion neurones capable of making fifty trillion connections (or synapses). Synapses hold thoughts, which become memories, and if we repeatedly use the same thought we create a strong memory. In turn, memories inform thoughts. So, simply put, by recalling positive memories we create positive thoughts.

But that starter supply of a hundred billion neurones, capable of fifty trillion different connections, is just the beginning. In the last fifteen years scientists have discovered that the number of synapses increases twentyfold by early adulthood, thereby creating over one thousand trillion connections. Nature is nothing if not economical: it doesn't produce surplus to requirements. It's simply given us a practically infinite capacity to learn and create.

I believe that this remarkable instrument that is the brain, properly used, is equipped to deal with virtually any challenge we face in life, with the exception of certain medical conditions. It can handle hundreds of thousands of actions simultaneously, it never stops working, it's the home of your thoughts, it subconsciously controls all your bodily processes, and it's capable of regeneration. Recent research into the ageing process has revealed that brain function does not deteriorate at anything like the rate previously imagined, and nor does old age impair the brain's capacity to learn. However, since the brain is made of flesh and blood, getting the best out of it means looking after it and using it, because the more you stimulate the brain the more its performance improves. Imagine that you could increase your brain performance by one degree, to 6 per cent of its capacity: it would then be operating 20 per cent more efficiently than the average brain. Now that would be an advantage, if ever there were one!

**Your life is what your thoughts make it.**
*Marcus Aurelius, (AD 121–80), Roman emperor*

Your brain determines your sense of well-being, and of confidence, your happiness and satisfaction. All these states reside in that complex organ, where neurotransmitters such as the endorphins maintain and increase these feelings and critically reduce your vulnerability to stress, your exposure to self-doubt. It follows, therefore, that if you can improve your thinking and your ability to use your brain, you will develop a winning outlook and a positive approach to your goals, which, in turn, will help you to achieve success. It's that simple.

But why is this important? It's important because the critical difference between successful individuals and the rest is not in the way they act, but in the way they think.

## Programming made easy

We have looked at how the brain stores all experience for future reference. When ancient man first discovered the secret of making fire, since survival depended on it, this skill was quickly learned. The brain automatically programmed itself to remember how the fire was made, and it's the same with other life skills that we take for granted. For example, think of those times when you got up in the night and had to make your way to a light switch on the opposite wall. In complete darkness you cross the room, and your hand automatically goes almost exactly to where you 'imagined' the light switch to be. The explanation is that, from your previous experiences of putting the light on or off in the room, you have subconsciously remembered the number of steps, the direction of the switch in relation to the bed and even the required angle of your arm.

Similarly, when you drive along a familiar route, it may sometimes feel as if no sooner have you turned the key in the ignition, then you have arrived at your destination – without any awareness at all of having thought about the process of getting there. This is due to the repetitive thought processes operating at the subconscious level – except, of course, when there is some sudden danger. At this point, thanks to the adrenaline response, we instantly override the subconscious process and take full control again.

The important thing to realise is that we can create within our subconscious the same kind of patterns that allow us to drive a familiar route automatically and find our way to the light-switch in the dark. It's possible to develop and program a habit of positive, success-oriented thought that operates, works for us, subconsciously twenty-four hours a day. And the means of doing this are not mysterious, but simple, powerful mental conditioning techniques. If the physical brain represents the hardware of a computer, then the way we think (the lifelong patterns we have created) is the software: that is, it can be recoded. And in changing the way we think we can unlearn those negative habits and patterns that have created the mechanisms that subconsciously cause us to fail in order to reinforce our negative self-image. Because as long as we *think* we'll fail, we will.

## Maintenance

So many people take their health for granted. They abuse their bodies through poor diet and lack of exercise, and compound the situation by drinking too much, smoking, and indulging in other forms of substance abuse. But the brain too is a physical organ, and the way we think can only be as effective as its capacity to function allows. So it is our personal responsibility to look after it.

Up until the 1990s it was believed that the brain, once formed, was unable to grow new cells. It is now accepted that brain cells are continually renewing themselves by increasing their connections to other cells. Since it is through these connections that thought travels, the more connections the brain is able to form the greater the function of the brain becomes. The size of the brain is not important in relation to intelligence – it doesn't matter whether you're the proud owner of a big brain or not. What counts is the number of connections between neurones, and the healthier the brain the greater its capacity for the cells to renew themselves and create new connections.

To help maximise your brain function for the rest of your life, look closely at your diet. There is an old saying, 'What's good for the heart is good for the head', which we should take as our motto in our task of creating maximum brain function. A good blood supply is critical for the brain: at any one time it requires 25 per cent of the blood pumped by the heart. Brain cells, like all other cells, require oxygen and energy. The only source of energy for the brain is blood glucose and as the brain cannot store its own energy it has to rely on a steady flow of energy-rich oxygenated blood to all parts of it. It follows that anything that impedes the efficiency of cerebral circulation has a direct effect on memory and concentration. This isn't a theory. It's a fact.

Low blood glucose, for example, can biochemically prevent the brain from storing new memories. It is known that one of the side effects of stress is an increased demand for nutrients. However, people under continual stress are more likely to try to manage their problem with alcohol, chocolate, nicotine or caffeine, substances that not only damage the cells and impede the brain's biochemistry but also affect its ability to successfully deal with stress itself, thereby creating a self-destructive pattern.

To maximise the well-being of your brain it's worth following certain basic guidelines – not as a one-off, six-week diet, but as a lifestyle change, because what we are talking about here is giving yourself optimal brain function for the rest of your life. How badly you want it is up to you, but stay with it once you've started and you'll be amazed by the rapid improvement you experience.

The rules are simple. Blood doesn't circulate as freely when there is excess fat in it, so choose low-fat foods. Don't go on a starvation diet; just eat less and more often and stick to low-calorie foodstuffs, unless you can burn off the extra calories through exercise. The starvation diet is a dangerous option because it radically reduces blood-glucose levels – and the brain's only fuel is glucose. So when you starve the body, you seriously risk starving the brain, and in extreme cases this can cause permanent damage.

Finally, it's always worth remembering that the brain uses glucose and cannot store fat so, although you may sometimes be sorely tempted, it is technically incorrect to call someone a fathead.

## Give yourself an upgrade

I am not an expert on brain function and I have never conducted scientific research. Nonetheless, I have seen at first hand many people radically improve their performances by changing the way they think about themselves, about their situation, and – critically – about their potential. For instance, often during my courses people will tell me they are right-brain or left-brain thinkers. Now, if you study more detailed accounts of brain anatomy than this book offers, you will discover that there are indeed differences between some people's brains and others – differences that explain, for example, why women tend to be more intuitive and men more practical, differences which doubtless find their roots in genetic evolution. And, of course, I do believe that some people are *naturally* more musical, artistic or creative, than others. But just as importantly I believe that those who do not consider themselves to have such gifts have, as we all do, the capacity to *develop* their musical, artistic and creative abilities. What stops them is thinking they can't, because if you label yourself a logical left-brain or an emotional right-brain person you are restricting your ability to 'see' yourself as anything other than that.

To do any real justice to the physiological basis of this subject would involve my going into far more detail than would be appropriate here, but I hope that this chapter has given you some insight into why and how the brain functions as it does. For it is really only when we start to understand how something works that we can begin to know how to make it work better.

I remember a very powerful charity campaign featuring a poster of a man with a fish, and the slogan said: 'Give this man a fish, and you feed his family for a day. Teach him to fish and he'll feed them for a lifetime.'

**I know of no more encouraging fact than the unquestionable ability of man to elevate his life by conscious endeavour.**
*Henry David Thoreau (1817–62), American writer and naturalist*

Of course, you can't change everything. When I was eighteen I got a summer job in Glasgow working in a bakery – or rather, in a factory that mass-produced bread. I was on permanent night shift, and while most of the process was automatic there were parts that had to be done manually. The hot rolls were loaded into wire baskets, which were then stacked on top of one another until they were twelve high. There wasn't much time to adjust the stack because of the speed with which the baskets kept arriving from the machine.

One evening an old fellow and I, both of us sweating profusely in the great heat of the place, were furiously loading these wire baskets. As usual, some of them were slightly misshapen, but none were unusable. On this occasion, though, as we stacked these less than perfect containers on top of one another, the tower they were making was becoming increasingly unstable. Both of us kept trying to make adjustments to stabilise it, and at some point a passing supervisor warned us that we would be in serious trouble if it fell. In the end we moved it away – by now it rather bore rather too close a resemblance to the Leaning Tower of Pisa – and started on the next one. But I couldn't disguise my concern (or was it panic?) at the thought of a reprimand from the supervisor. To which, with considerable wisdom, the old man responded, 'We've done our best. It's the baskets that need fixing, not us. If it falls,' he added stoically, 'it falls.'

We must recognise the need to do our best, but accept those limitations and restrictions that are beyond our control; and, importantly, we must recognise the difference, between things we can change and things we can't.

**Watch your thoughts; they become words.**
**Watch your words; they become actions.**
**Watch your actions; they become habits.**
**Watch your habits; they become character.**
**Watch your character; it becomes your destiny.**
*Frank Outlaw*

# 3 You the Hero

## You're unique

As children we are so often told of the uniqueness of snowflakes, that no two are exactly the same. We are told the same of our fingerprints, of our voices, of our DNA; so we can take it for certain that each and every one of us is a unique individual. Yet despite our understanding that never in the history of the world has somebody quite like us existed, we habitually compare ourselves with others. We use them as yardsticks against which to measure our success. How often have you read in a newspaper of somebody who's achieved great things, then quickly checked that they *are* actually older than you, thereby giving yourself at least some temporary reassurance that you may yet equal their success.

But comparing yourself with other people is a meaningless exercise because you will never know what *their* motivators are, what drives *them*, what abilities *they* have that are unique to them. There will always be skills that others have that you wish you had; equally *you* have skills that other people wish they had. We often, wrongly, assume that skills must be musical, artistic or intellectual to be of any great value, while in reality we all have marvellous gifts, integral parts of our make-up, that we continually overlook, such as compassion, patience, humour, understanding, the gift of communication – all of them strong tools that we can use to help us achieve future success.

In the end, continually comparing yourself with others can only adversely affect your self-image, your self-belief and your ability to achieve. The person whose gifts you should examine to see if they are being fully exploited is you.

**Our self-image and our habits tend to go together. Change one, and you automatically change the other.**
*Maxwell Maltz (1899–1975)*

We are all unique as individuals, but what I think makes us unique as a species is our ability to bring about change in ourselves through the exercise of conscious thought. Our awareness of who we are, where we are and where we want to go is what gives us this extraordinary position in the world.

Scientists now believe that 50 per cent of personality and ability is inherited through our genes – which means that 50 per cent of it is not. And that 50 per cent it is up to us to create and develop. What would you most like to change if you could? Of course, we must accept that there are things we were born with that no amount of positive thinking is going to change – our height, our eye and skin colour, and so on. But we can change the way we think about them, and this is a uniquely powerful quality. So often I come across people who say, 'Oh, I'm nobody special.' The reality is that everyone is somebody special, but if you do not believe it it's a certainty that no one else will.

Think of a child in infancy. She receives an enormous amount of praise and unconditional love, she's told how special she is – positive reinforcing messages to the developing mind. But as we get older this process slows down. One particularly significant factor here is that we learn to conform, to fit in; we don't want to stand out from the crowd when we go out to play, we don't want to be different from other children; we become nobody special. So the conforming process is something we teach ourselves in childhood. It's a time that determines the development of our self-image, and later in life we seek to stay within the boundaries of that image because it is safe. We forget that we have the ability to change.

The same is true of the corporate world: here too we find resistance to change and a pattern of imitation. When we look at the car-hire or the fast-food business, say, it seems to us at first that the individual companies are virtually indistinguishable; but on closer examination we discover small distinctions – in branding, customer care, integrity – that have become their unique selling-points and give them their crucial competitive advantage. Companies that ultimately succeed have learned that the small details make the big difference. They have branded themselves as having a unique identity, an identification with a product or perhaps with an aspect of their customer service.

And in a sense you are no different. You can do the same if you choose to identify what is unique about you: you can create your own special brand. Try this exercise: think of an organisation or person that you can describe in one word. For a person you might choose 'funny', 'humble', 'thoughtless'; for an organisation it might be 'ruthless', 'incompetent', 'visionary' – whatever. Now think of one positive word to describe one aspect of yourself that you're proud of. This is the first step towards identifying yourself – not only who you are, but who you want to become. Small details make the big difference.

## Individuality

Your individuality is your sense of who you are. If you have a clear image of who you are, you will not allow yourself to be defined by labels. Don't define yourself by the job you do, the house you live in, the car you drive, or the clothes you wear. You are *not* the sum total of these things. It is in themselves that successful people believe.

Their potential to succeed is dependent not on status or labels but on a quiet confidence that they have it in themselves to get where they want to go.

**Death is not the greatest loss in life. The greatest loss in life is what dies inside us while we live.**
*Norman Cousins (1915–90), American humanitarian and writer*

A certain bishop was lying on his deathbed. He reflected to his wife, 'When I was a young man I was determined to change the world, so I went around telling everyone how they should live and what they should do. 'But,' he went on, 'it didn't seem to make any difference because no one really listened to me. So I decided I would change my family instead; but, to my dismay, even they didn't pay any attention or make the changes I wanted for them.' He paused and sighed. 'Only now,' he said, 'in the last years of my life, have I recognised that the only person upon whom I could exert any real influence was me. If I wanted to change the world, I should have begun with myself.'

Whatever your ambitions in life, the road to success and achievement is a road you walk alone. Yes, you can travel alongside others on the path you tread – your team-mates, family, or colleagues – but ultimately, it's a solo journey. No one else can take the steps for you.

Similarly, if you want to be a winner, whatever your field of endeavour, it is you and you alone who must make the effort to get there. It is through the exploitation of your natural gifts that your goal will be realised. Nobody can lose weight for you, nobody can get fit for you – you have to accept personal responsibility. To be an individual does not mean being isolated – it's about identifying who you are and choosing what you want to be. And it's this that gives you a potential for success that you could never previously have dreamt of. When I first started researching personal development, I thought that claims of guaranteed success were 'too American' because they seemed to offer too much too easily – instant wealth, instant satisfaction. In fact the methodologies offered none of those things. What they revealed was this: you determine what it is you want to achieve, and your power to do so lies in recognising as much. Only you can determine what *your* success is. Making the commitment to achieving it doesn't guarantee that success. But not making it does guarantee failure.

## Recognise opportunity

> People are always blaming their circumstances for what they are. I don't believe in circumstances. The people who get on in this world are the people who get up and look for the circumstances they want and, if they can't find them, make them.
> *George Bernard Shaw (1856–1950)*

Success begins with one person seizing an opportunity and working hard to turn that opportunity into success. But the first step is to recognise the opportunity for what it is, and that can simply be a matter of perception.

There was an old priest who lived in a valley. For forty years he looked after all the people who lived in his parish. He conducted the baptisms and the funerals, married the young couples, comforted the sick and the lonely. For all that time he was the perfect example of a good and holy person. Then one day it began to rain, and it rained and rained in biblical proportions until after twenty days of non-stop downpour the water was so high that the old priest was forced to get up on to the chapel roof. There he sat shivering when a man came along in a rowing-boat and said, 'Father, quick, get in and I will take you to the high ground.'

The priest looked at him and answered, 'For forty years I've done everything God expected of me and, I hope, maybe a little more. I've done the baptisms and the funerals, I've comforted the sick and the lonely, I only ever take one week's holiday a year. And when I have that week's holiday, do you know what I do? I go to an orphanage and I help the cook. I have great faith in God because this is the God that I serve, so you can go with your boat and I will stay. My God will save me.'

The man in the boat left. Two more days passed and the rains reached such a level that the old priest was clinging to the very top of the steeple as the waters swirled around him. Then a helicopter arrived and the pilot called to him, 'Father, quick, we'll send down a winch. Put the harness around you and we'll take you to safety', to which the old priest replied, 'No, no', and again he gave his speech about his life's work and his faith in God. So the helicopter left, and some hours later the priest was swept away and drowned.

Being a good man, he went straight to heaven. Furious at his fate, he arrived there in a very bad mood. He was squelching angrily through heaven when all of a sudden he came upon God. And an astonished God it was who looked at him and said, 'Father Macdonald! What a surprise!' At which the priest stared at Him and said, 'Oh! A surprise, is it? For forty years I did everything you ever asked of me and more, and in my moment of greatest need you let me drown.'

And God stared back at him, bewildered: 'You drowned? I can't believe that – I'm sure I sent you a boat and a helicopter.'

The reality is that the boats and helicopters of opportunity are there in our lives all the time. We just have to recognise them for what they are, and we can only really do this when we have set ourselves an objective. It's only then that these apparently random occurrences, which we would normally have been blind to, will be evident as the opportunities that they are. Almost every event creates an opportunity. There are exceptions, of course – personal tragedies such as bereavement. But we should try to accept these as facts of life, events over which we have no control, and allow ourselves to grieve. What we mustn't do is use them as excuses for doing nothing.

**I skate to where I think the puck will be.**
*Wayne Gretzsky*

Whatever your life circumstances, your starting-point is not an indicator of where you are capable of going. An immigrant to the United Kingdom is four times as likely to become a self-made millionaire as someone born here. Many self-made millionaires left school without formal qualifications. The essential point is that success has very little to do with background. It has a great deal more to do with your self-belief and your ability to recognise an opportunity.

Your frame of mind is crucially important in determining how open you are to identifying good breaks that come your way. If you are in a negative frame of mind or have a poor self-image, if you don't believe you will be successful, then you are unlikely to recognise opportunities, and there is nothing in life so regretted as missed opportunities.

**There is never a wrong time to do the right thing.**
*Anon.*

Indeed, I believe that the real tragedy in life is not failing to reach our goals, but not having goals to aspire to. I sometimes hear people say, 'I don't get breaks, I'm just not a lucky person.' What's happened is that they've closed their minds to the chances around them; like the old priest, they're blind to the boats and helicopters. So don't wait to take those opportunities, don't put it off until tomorrow; don't end up at the age of eighty-five wishing you had done all those things that you have the chance to start doing today.

**Save worry and anxiety for the major upsets in life. Today make a conscious effort to see something positive in every situation.**

*Anon.*

## Your past does *not* determine your future

You have no doubt occasionally met someone who says, 'It's just the way it is', 'That's my lot', or 'Nothing so fortunate ever happens to me.' It has been said that if you do what you've always done, you'll get what you've always got. Our thinking habits subconsciously determine how we think, how we respond and how we act. Believing that you've always been a failure only works if you hold firmly to the belief. But you *can* break out of that conviction, if you choose to do so. I said earlier that anything you believe to be true about yourself is understood at a subconscious level. Furthermore, your subconscious mind cannot distinguish fact from fiction, and will continually seek to reinforce whatever subconscious image you have of yourself by encouraging actions that confirm it, or inhibiting actions that would contradict it. You only have to look at the effects of hypnosis to know this is true.

It's interesting how often, when friends get together, they reminisce about the past: the good times, parties, holidays, moments of shared experience. Yet as individuals facing new opportunities, we regularly focus on the things at which we've failed – thus creating fear for what may happen in the future. Collectively we tend to remember the positive; alone, the negative – so we resist change. But change is the one constant in our lives; to try to resist change is ultimately to sow the seeds of personal failure.

And this is equally true at a corporate level.

It is an astonishing statistic that 40 per cent of the UK's FT index companies of 1980 had ceased to exist by 1990, and the same was true of the Fortune 500 companies America. The number one reason amongst the many contributing factors was that they hadn't changed. They hadn't kept up with their customers. They just kept doing what they had always done, neither evolving nor anticipating developments in their customers' needs. They were paralysed in the security of their past.

The past has gone; we can't change it. And we must accept that as change occurs we too must change. Yet often when people are offered a promotion, the new responsibility and expectation create anxiety. When asked to change, they resist. They are being asked to do something which, judging from past experiences, they don't believe they are capable of doing. Rather like the beautiful caged bird – all its life imprisoned, fed and watered by its owner. The day the owner dies a neighbour comes along, opens the cage door and says to the bird, 'OK, now have your freedom.' But the bird stands in the doorway of the cage, looks all around and thinks to itself, 'I'll just stay here, because this is the world I know, and for all its limitations I'm safe here.' But what the beautiful bird doesn't realise is that outside the cage is a world to be explored, a fantastic world of opportunities.

How many of us have gone for a job interview convinced that we're terrible at interviews, recalling on the way there all the stored-up memories of the times we've been turned down? This rehashing of old failures unconsciously creates an emotional response in the form of stress, which manifests itself in headaches, irritability, and a hundred and one other ways. The more stressed we become the more likely we are to create a self-fulfilling prophecy by giving a poor account of ourselves at the interview, so that when the bad news comes through we can say with complete conviction, 'I knew I'd never get that job!'

> **Good people are good because they've come to wisdom through failure. We get very little wisdom from success, you know.**
> *William Saroyan (1908–81), American playwright and novelist*

Let me share another story with you. I played golf for my university. Now, I have a unique record there because before my final game I had played twenty-one matches and I'd lost twenty-one. Just before my last full game as a student I remember thinking, 'I'd like one victory before I leave.' The team captain told me the opponent I was going to play had a handicap of 12 – my handicap at the time was 7 – so I thought I had a good chance. I teed up against him as the last match out. He hit a wonderful drive and, surprisingly, I followed with a wonderful drive of my own. We both made par at the first and the second; at the third hole he went one up and stayed one up until I got it back at the ninth; by the tenth hole we were both only two over par, playing the most extraordinarily good golf. We got to the fourteenth, where I levelled the game; at the fifteenth I went one up; we tied the sixteenth.

As we walked towards the seventeenth hole I said to this fellow, 'Where do you play your golf?' He mentioned a championship golf course. I was amazed, and when I asked him how that had come about, he told me he used to play for Cambridge University first team. Now, to play for Cambridge University first team you need a very low handicap, certainly a lot better than 12. Puzzled, I asked him what his handicap was. 'Two,' he said. You see it appears that my short-sighted captain had read 2 as 12 (or, more likely, he had had too much wine at lunchtime). The minute I realised this man's handicap was 2 and not 12 my confidence left me and all the memories of losing flooded back in.

Needless to say, I didn't disappoint my subconscious mind and I lost the seventeenth and ultimately the eighteenth hole – my hundred-per-cent record for defeat at golf intact. As long as I'd believed I could win, I'd had a winning manner about me – the way I walked, thought and played. But the minute I believed I was going to lose, everything changed.

*

Being a champion means thinking like a champion. Winners win because they visualise the rewards of success; losers lose because they visualise the penalties of failure.

How many times have you committed yourself to getting fit, improving your health and well being through a new fitness regime? And how many times have you failed? When you reflect on past failures, you are consciously reinforcing memories of failure, and in so doing creating the conditions for your new well intentioned initiative to fail. The fact is you can achieve anything realistic you put your mind to. But you have to believe that you can achieve it, and that means changing a habit of thought. A habit is simply a pattern of behaviour subconsciously enacted. Habits can be learned, habits can be unlearned – in as little as twenty-one days. Think about this: in the morning when you get up, which shoe do you put on first? If you think about it, you may realise that you always put the same one on first. Let's suppose it's the right one. Stick a note in your bedroom that you'll see first thing in the morning: 'Put left shoe on first today.' Now do what the note says, every day for twenty-one days, and then take the note down. You will be amazed to discover that you are now automatically putting on your left shoe first, through the conscious forming of a new unconscious habit.

Often in business you challenge the way something is done, only to be hold, 'Well, that's the way we've always done it.' It seems to me that this is often the best reason for changing it. I remember a professor of business management who was in charge of his small department's office expenditure once telling me that one day he'd noticed that his secretary had bought twelve pairs of scissors. When he asked her why, she replied, 'Because my predecessor always did.' It turned out that in the days before computers, when speeches and notes were being written a lot of cutting and pasting went on. No one had stopped to think, when this procedure was no longer necessary, that they didn't need those twelve pairs of scissors any more.'

In business, work habits and ways of doing things that once seemed sensible are often transformed over time into pointless exercises. We must always ask the question 'Why are we doing this?', and if we don't like the answer we should make a definite commitment to changing that procedure. There is always another way of doing something. In a more general sense, recognise that the learned patterns of behaviour that you employ are shaping your future. If you want those patterns to continue, leave them as they are. But if you're not happy with them, then you have the choice and the ability to start the process of change right now. Complacency, indifference, and procrastination are your major enemies.

## Dream big

Everything begins with a dream, so dream big. But don't expect to get there in a single leap (leave that to Superman). We are all familiar with the old Confucian proverb: 'Even the longest journey begins with one small step.' So commit yourself to the journey you are about to make and take that first step. Because if you don't, that journey will never begin and the dream will stay just that. A dream that isn't followed by action is an idle wish. A dream that generates action can change the world. Furthermore, you are capable of creating any future scenario you want, so don't limit yourself to small dreams and small ambitions. If you aim big and come up short you are still going to be a lot further along than you had thought possible.

**The fountain of contentment must spring up in the mind. He who has so little knowledge of human nature as to seek happiness by changing anything**

**but his own disposition will waste his life in
fruitless efforts and multiply the grief which he
purposes to remove.**

*Samuel Johnson*

I am inspired by the example of Terry Fox, a young Canadian, who was diagnosed with bone cancer and had to have his leg removed in order to prevent the spread of the disease. Moved by the suffering of other cancer patients, he determined to run across Canada to raise money for research. With the support of the Canadian Cancer Society, Terry began training for the 'Marathon of Hope'. On 12 April 1980, in a farewell gesture, he dipped his artificial leg in the Atlantic Ocean and left St John's, Newfoundland, with a target of twenty-six miles a day. Capturing the imagination of a nation, his run was closely followed in the media.

Terry's dream was to raise $100,000. 'I guess that one of the most important things I've learned is that nothing is ever completely bad. Even cancer. It made me a better person. It has given me courage and a sense of purpose that I never had before. But you don't have to do like I did – wait until you lose a leg or get some awful disease – before you take the time to find out what kind of stuff you're really made of. You can start now. Anybody can.'

One hundred and forty-three days and 3,339 miles later, on the outskirts of Thunder Bay, Ontario, Terry stopped running. The cancer had spread to his lungs. But by 1 February 1981, when the Terry Fox Marathon of Hope Fund totalled $24.17 million, his dream of raising $1 for every person in Canada had been realised. On 28 June, one month short of his twenty-third birthday, Terry Fox died. Every September since then, at points all around the world, his legacy has been celebrated with the Terry Fox Run. The foundation has raised over $180 million, in the Rockies a mountain has been named after him, and there is a huge memorial outside Thunder Bay. Terry Fox inspired millions.

Three days after his death a journalist wrote, 'Terry Fox's race is over. In fact, he never finished the course; none of us ever do. What is important is the running. What is important is to set goals. What is important is not to quit, not ever. What is important is to run well and honestly, with as much human grace as possible – not forgetting, too, to take joy in the running, to laugh at life's absurdities as well as weep at its cruelties.'

Terry Fox dreamt big. All winners dream big. The kind of dream I'm talking about, of course, is the conscious kind, the kind that we control. All of us have day-dreamed, consciously created a fantasy situation in our minds. We should daydream more, because it's the activity that underpins the visualisation techniques that are an important aspect of realising our goals, and that we shall discuss in more detail later.

It is also very important, I believe, when you have a dream, not to share it with people I think of as dream-stealers, people who undermine your ambitions, who say, 'You can't do that. What are you playing at? You're bound to fail!' It's vital to share your dreams only with people who fully believe in you and your ambitions, who will be catalysts, encouraging you at those inevitable times when you feel disheartened and negative.

Dreams work for individuals, and they work for business. Under Jack Welch, the chairman and chief executive officer of General Electric, the American company has become the biggest in the world. He has always had a great belief in setting ambitious goals – dreaming big, having ambitious targets: ' "Stretch" in its simplest form says nothing is impossible, and the setting of stretch targets inspires people and catches their imagination. Stretch means using dreams to set business targets with no real idea of how to get there, and as soon as we become sure we can do it, it is time for another stretch.'

I know of athletes who for years have visualised standing on the winner's podium in the Olympic stadium. Indeed, I believe that every Olympic gold-medallist has already long before the day of triumph so strongly visualised winning that when they get to the podium it seems familiar.

The subconscious mind will always move towards the image you hold of yourself – which includes your goals. If you are convinced in yourself that you will realise your goals, you will create the conditions which must assist your progress. Equally if you are convinced that something bad is going to happen you will create the circumstances that will allow you to become discouraged and lose confidence when some unexpected challenge is encountered. You will see such occurences as failures you had anticipated – and identify with them. People who habitually fail have a powerful failure mentality. They have encoded into their subconscious the belief that they will not succeed and unconsciously follow a pattern of behaviour that fits in with that belief. Those who succeed, by contrast, have a powerful success mentality. Usually without realising it, they have encoded in their subconscious the image of future success. So it's important, when you are setting goals for the future – when you dream of the victories that lie ahead – that you think positively and dream big.

## Become your own coach

It sometimes strikes people as odd that sportsmen such as Tiger Woods, one of the best golfers in the world, and Pete Sampras, one of the best tennis players in the world, have personal coaches. If they are the best in the world in their fields, what can anybody possibly teach them! The point is, of course, that like many peak performers, they understand that a coach serves many functions: to encourage them at times when they are feeling down, to help them look for strategies that will give them the competitive edge that they have found in the past and that they know they can recreate in the future, to help put them in the right frame of mind – a winning frame of mind. But just as important is the coach's talent for praising, for reinforcing the positive images of victory that allow them to stay at the top of their chosen professions.

As a child learns to feed himself, his parents do their best, in spite of the mess that he makes in the process, to unreservedly praise him. In the work environment, companies that let a blame culture emerge never develop highly motivated, powerfully driven staff. To guard against this happening within their company, some years ago Toyota put in place a number of measures for its managers to take, two of which were particularly striking. The first was the one just mentioned: don't criticise, praise. If someone does something wrong, praise him – that way he won't be afraid to make mistakes or to tell you what went wrong, and this will enable you to find a way of making improvements. Second, Toyota asked the staff to be open about any complaints they might have about their managers. So the appraisal system now worked both ways. The staff appraised the managers, the managers the senior managers, the senior managers the directors, and so on – it kept everybody on their toes, but it also encouraged everyone to do better.

Encouragement is vital when you set out on the path towards becoming a natural born winner. It is essential that you put into your subconscious mind positive images, positive expressions and positive statements that relate to you as a success. One of the qualities of coaches is that they are enthusiastic. Enthusiasm is very difficult to fake, and nobody can give it to you. But if you believe in your goal enthusiasm will be the automatic con-comitant, because belief and commitment demand it. If you run into difficulties recall not your failures but your past successes, and hold these memories in your mind. Reaffirm your future goal. Get into the habit of thinking positively, praising yourself when you do something well. Reaffirm the experience by saying to yourself, 'Well done! Good!'

Affirmations are expressions that allow you to reinforce an already positive self-image. They act as triggers to your subconscious mind, helping to strengthen the image of the person you are seeking to become. The French pharmacist and psychotherapist Émile Coué, who practised about the turn of the twentieth century, used to tell his patients to say out loud: 'Every day in every way I'm getting better and better.' When he compared these patients post-operatively with other patients who used no such formula, he found that his patients did indeed recover much faster than the others.

Think of some affirmations that will work for you. Whatever you choose, keep them simple. They must always be in the first person and relate to a future state that you are moving towards, for instance, 'I am becoming healthier now', 'I am actively moving towards my goal now', 'I am becoming calmer every day'. Say them to yourself throughout the day, out loud. And don't worry about feeling self-conscious – it will be worth it, because it *will* work. You can often see athletes before a critical moment getting themselves fully prepared. They go through a ritual of settling their nerves and telling themselves 'I can do this', 'I'm ready', 'This is the one'. Watch their lips; watch the results.

> **The artist is nothing without the gift, but the gift is nothing without work**
> *Émile Zola (1840–1902), French novelist and critic*

Imagine you are coaching your best friend, someone you love dearly, who depends on you entirely to help her achieve an ambition. How would you go about it? Think about it, and then apply that same approach to yourself. If you are planning now to achieve certain changes in your life, don't be afraid to seek assistance. Look to people you admire, who have done what *you* are trying to do. Ask them how they did it, what pitfalls to watch out for, about the disappointments that they encountered and how they overcame them. Even at the highest levels, advice can help.

After winning a number of PGA tour events, Nick Faldo, as an extremely gifted young professional golfer, approached the golf teacher David Leadbetter to ask him to help him develop a new swing that would stand up to the pressures of world-class golf and bring him major championships. It was a very brave thing to do – people thought he was crazy, committing professional suicide – but he believed that if he was going to achieve his aim he had no choice, and he set about rebuilding his swing. He went on to win three British Opens and three US Masters titles.

If you go through life vaguely hoping for the best but preparing for the worst, the worst is what you'll get. If, on the other hand, you are *determined* to achieve the best, then it is up to you to give yourself every chance to do exactly that. Work out the plan you want to follow, become your own coach, encourage yourself constantly, and when you come up against difficulties ask for help. This is all you have to do. Seek, and ye shall find – you will be amazed how many people will gladly help you on your journey.

## Overcome the failure habit

When I was a young man, and as far back as my schooldays, I always believed I would fail, that I wouldn't pass the crucial exams. This was caused by a number of factors that I now recognise. I allowed myself to be easily discouraged when I made a mistake. I identified myself with failure; I didn't see myself as simply lacking the knowledge or understanding. One thing I was certain of was that I wouldn't get into university. When I was sixteen, six weeks before our chemistry 'O' level, the science teacher went through the register one at a time, predicting who would get a grade A or a grade B; when he came to me, he just said, 'You're going to fail; you're wasting your time. You're not going to pass anything.' I remember being enraged by this, by his insensitivity, by his almost bullying satisfaction – and if his intention was to galvanise me into doing something, it certainly worked. Off I went to the bookshop and bought myself *Teach Yourself Chemistry* and the course books for years 1, 2 and 3 – I was currently on year 4. Then I spent two weeks putting myself through it, from the basic structure of the atom up to the fourth-year syllabus work. I took the 'O' level, and not only did I pass but I scored a grade B, which meant I had achieved 60–69 per cent. I was going to university after all, I decided. The news generated some rather wonderful facial expressions among the teachers, but two years later I fulfilled my ambitions.

Up until that point in my life, all the things at which I had believed I would fail I *had* failed at. I had predicted, in very clear terms to myself months if not years before, that failure was inevitable; often I would tell others that I didn't believe something I hoped for would materialise. Accordingly, it never did.

What I had mistaken as some vague sense of personal destiny became in fact a self-fulfilling prophecy. I had programmed my subconscious mind to expect failure; in fact, it demanded failure. The wonderful workings of the brain enabled it to fulfil my negative expectations. Every time a failure that I had predicted became reality, it reinforced my belief that it was my lot in life to fail, and that there was nothing I could do about it.

It wasn't until the life-changing wake-up call of being diagnosed with Hodgkin's disease that I determined never again to allow myself to think like this. I now knew that I was fully responsible for the way I thought. My habit of believing failure to be inevitable had been the very cause of my failure. I had been safely ensconced in a cage of my own making; getting out of my comfort zone had been just too damned hard, too scary. The changes I had wanted to make, I hadn't wanted to be responsible for

– I'd wanted them just to happen. I'd wanted to wake up and find my world OK.

Failure is not about losing, it's about repeating a pattern of behaviour that you feel comfortable with. If I asked you how you feel when you fail, what would you reply? Would you make an excuse, or maybe mutter a resigned acceptance? How do you justify your failures? Many people just make a joke of it, as though they don't really care. But it is important that you do care because, once you care enough, that will become your trigger. It will be the catalyst that helps you to start making real changes.

Your past failures are events that happened in the past. They are not what you are about; they are not labels that you should stick to yourself and forever identify with. They are just things that happened – learn the lesson.

> **Each problem that I solved became a rule which served afterwards to solve other problems.**
> *René Descartes*

Any change we make in our lives has to follow a natural order of progression. It's very much like learning to run. We have to learn to crawl, to stand, and to walk first: there are no short cuts. And if we determine that we are going to succeed, we must learn how to break the failure habits we have spent a lifetime learning.

How do we do this?

Identify the point at which your personal failure mechanism starts to kick in. Normally it starts with saying something negative or visualising the inevitability of defeat. Memories of previous failures start to weaken your determination.

Stop using negative talk – 'I can't', 'I won't', 'I'm not able to'. Speak positively when you refer to your future goals, when you speak about yourself, *and* about other people. And remember that just as habits are learned, so they can be unlearned.

# Find the hero within

What is a hero? I think a hero is someone who does something that he or she is naturally afraid to do, someone who does a thing that requires courage. Heroes are people we admire for their actions, and whose qualities represent to us an ideal. To many young boys their father is a hero. He is perceived as brave, fearless and strong – all qualities that young boys aspire to. And the interesting thing is that children *believe* that they can be just as heroic. It's not just demonstrated by the kinds of games they play. Remember that 96 per cent of four-year-olds have high self-esteem; they believe they can do anything they want to. But by the time they are eighteen, fewer than 5 per cent still have that high self-esteem. So what happened to these children to make them lose their sense of self-worth? Research has shown that on average parents speak to, rebuke or instruct their children in the negative form 90 per cent of the time. Given that the average 12-year-old is conservatively estimated to have received over one hundred thousand negative soundbites during their life, it's easy to see how inadvertently a child's self-image can suffer. Although no parent knowingly seeks to undermine their child's confidence or self-esteem, the demands made on parents often mean that they are unable to sit down and explain their actions to the child. But the effects of praise versus blame culture – or the positive versus negative approach – can be clearly seen in terms of the developing self-image. Then add to this the negative messages coming from school and peer groups – 'You can't do this', 'You can't sing', 'You're stupid.' Any child, whether he is particularly impressionable or averagely resilient, if he hears enough criticisms about himself, will end up believing them. And the image of himself that forms in his mind will be based on them.

But the amazing thing is that, despite all this, the memory of that potential, that self-belief, remain within us. I believe that within every person there is a hero, a dormant hero with whom we have lost contact. That hero had absolute conviction in his ability to succeed. And the success we're talking about isn't to do with winning bravery awards or getting medals for acts of courage on the battlefield – it's about being able to stand up every time you fall down, and to believe that no matter how often you fall down, you have the determination to get up one more time. As was succintly expressed to me whilst I was training for an endurance event: a winner is simply someone who got up one more time than he fell down.

It is very important that we reconnect with those positive self-images of our childhood, because when we do we reinforce them at a subconscious level. And every time we achieve something that we would naturally shy away from, we are forming a powerful positive memory, building a stronger self-belief, and further expanding the limits of our horizon.

When I was lying in my hospital bed after my operation, awaiting the results of the various tests they were running, I started to imagine my funeral and, more specifically, the tributes my friends would be paying to me. I must admit that my imagination came up with some quite wonderful eulogies, expounding on my many extraordinary achievements. This got me thinking, later, that we should always design our lives back to front. Think of the things you would like to be said of you at the end of your life, think of the things you would like to have achieved, and no matter how exceptional they may be, go for them. Write the obituary you would like to be proudest of, and set about making it happen now.

> **Live as you will wish to have lived when you are dying.**
>
> *Charles F. Geller*

The thing about heroes is that in fact they are ordinary everyday people like you and me – they just do things that to us appear extraordinary. When we face the things in our lives that we are afraid of and that hold us back, and overcome them, we are performing acts of private heroism. And they vastly improve our self-image along the way.

I have a godson called Finn. When he was four years old his father Tom and I took him for a picnic. When we came to a small river that had to be crossed with the aid of stepping-stones, because of Finn's age and lack of confidence Tom picked him up and carried him. On the way back, Tom again carried him across. I hung about on the other side of the river and, for a joke, called to him, 'Finn, Finn, come and get me, I'm afraid of the water.' Finn turned to his father, expecting him to do something. Tom, though, playing along, pretended that he was in a hurry to get back to the car. 'We'll have to leave Robin behind,' he said, and walked off. Finn watched his father disappear, and then looked at me. 'Don't leave me, Finn,' I said. Suddenly his face became a mask of concentration – his two little hands formed into fists and he began to prepare himself to cross the river. He planted his foot on the first stepping-stone, at which point I ran across to stop him going any further. If a child of four, I realised then, could find within himself the resources to overcome what was probably a considerable fear in order to help somebody, then what greater power adults must possess when they face their fears and overcome them.

It's taking the first step that seems so hard. But take it, no matter how small, because it's that step that will start you on your journey to whatever goal you have set yourself. It's a short step. And only you can take it.

# 4   The Big Secret

I remember as a boy reading of alchemists who hoped to turn lead into gold. They were probably the first people to seek the lazy man's way to riches – which I imagine is the title of some book somewhere. I mean the type you see advertised in the backs of magazines, books with appealing titles such as *How to Make Money While You Sleep*, or *Ninety Days to Your First Million*. The only people who ever got rich from those adverts, probably, are the people who place them.

No doubt many of us would love to discover a magic bullet, a recipe for success; a Holy Grail that after years of searching is found upon a mountain top and bestows upon its finder great happiness, joy and wealth.

> **Just think how happy you would be if you lost everything you have right now, and then got it back again.**
>
> *Anon.*

But after many years of meditating on a mountain top (all right, a table top) I have finally discovered the big secret, and I can no longer keep it from the world. I am prepared for the first time to reveal what it is: *there is no secret*.

The pointlessness of looking for a single solution is well illustrated by this little story. One evening, in a small village, a man is to be seen on his hands and knees under a street light. A second man comes along and asks him what the matter is. 'Oh,' he replies, 'I've dropped my key.' The second man also gets down on his hands and knees, and starts to help. After two minutes of fruitless searching, he turns to the first man: 'Where did you drop the key?' The first man points down the road into the darkness and says, 'Down there.' 'Well then,' the second man says, 'why are we looking here?' 'Oh,' replies the first man, 'because the light's much better here.'

The first man's response is to look in the place he feels safe, no matter how wrong that place is, no matter that he will not find his key there however long he searches. To find it he would have to look outside his self-imposed comfort zone. Unconsciously, he would rather sacrifice his chances of ever finding the key than stray outside the area that he perceives as safe.

It's also, in a sense, like the man in the middle of a forest – looking for the forest. If he would only take the time to climb a tree and look around him, he would see that he's already found it.

So there is no secret. But I do believe there are straightforward principles that are common to those who have enjoyed and continue to enjoy success.

## The way of the winner

It seems to be natural for us to think of winners exclusively as those who win the race, come top of the list, cross the line in first position, and as a result find themselves on the champion's podium. The old saying 'No one remembers who comes second' shows how we tend to devalue the individual achievements of all the other runners. But the reality is that winners come in all shapes and sizes.

Winners have this in common: they have achieved their goal, they have climbed their own personal Everest and felt good about themselves; this means that they have pushed themselves a little bit more. But those who come second, third, fifth or whatever should not think of themselves as losers. Somebody once said to me: 'Show me a good loser and I'll show you a loser'. This may be one perspective on it, but it certainly isn't one that I have found common amongst winners, who have often encountered failure along the way but have found the strength to pick themselves up again.

Winners see themselves as winners, and they think accordingly. They don't identify themselves with their failures; rather, they see them as lessons to be learned from, then get on with applying those lessons in the future. Winners recognise that success and failure are not destinations in themselves, but experiences in the journey of life. There is a mind-set, I believe, common to winners: whatever they are engaged in, they persist; they live in the present; they don't spend their time forever recalling former glories *or* past failures. They look forward to their future achievements and, recognising opportunities by virtue of the fact they have set themselves a goal, they will go the extra yard.

Everyone was born with an inherent capacity to be a winner. See yourself as a winner, because every victory along the way, no matter how small, will give you the confidence to go on to greater successes.

I recently came across a poem that told the story of a young boy competing in a school race. The boy was determined to come first in order to impress his father, but during the race he fell over four times and so came in last. As he crossed the line, he received an exceptionally large cheer from the crowd and a hug from his father. He was confused by this response, until his father explained to him that winning was no more than this: getting up again each time you fall. The boy had risen four times and carried on, and in his father's eyes, and no doubt in the eyes of the others who had cheered him, he was a winner.

Remember that winning is very much to do with having a winning mind-set, a winning attitude. You don't have to come first every time, but you must always believe that you can, you must always give it your best shot.

# What do successful people have in common?

As children learning to walk and talk, we imitate our parents – hence the old expression, 'Monkey see, monkey do.' When we're older, we spend large sums on magazines that show us the cooking methods of our favourite chefs so that we can copy them; we pore over fashions in the glossies and imitate what we see there; we study our sporting heroes and emulate their techniques, hoping to gain improvement from the tricks of the trade. In the same way, if you want to be successful it would be wise to imitate the patterns common to successful people. If you wish to create a model for personal success, you can't do better than to study those who enjoy success, whether at personal, team, corporate or entrepreneurial level. Because although no two people or businesses are ever exactly the same, the essential ingredients remain constant.

When I was a young man, mad keen on golf, I read everything I could find about the latest theories on the golf swing and its dynamics, sent off for every gimmick going, and applied them with an evangelical passion. This game was to be mastered and, lacking the talent, I was going to use science to help me do so. The deeper I went into my researches, though, and the more technical my interpretation of the perfect golf swing became, the further I got from striking the ball well. It was my father who saved me, every time, by bringing me back to the basics of grip, stance, tempo and swing. I have often thought of this experience when speaking at business conferences where results and performance have been endlessly scrutinised, analysed in the minutest detail, in the hope of providing insights and solutions in the pursuit of success.

But the fact is that the basic ingredients of achievement are neither complex nor obscure. Successful individuals operate four natural success principles, often without any awareness that this is what they are doing. Some, of course, emphasise one aspect much more than others – indeed, no two ever use exactly the same combination. But, rather like different chefs cooking omelettes, though the taste and texture of the finished products may differ, they will all contain the same ingredients.

The four natural principles for success are:

A clear goal
A definite plan
Confidence
No fear of failure.

## A clear goal

Both teams in a football match know that the object of their endeavours is to score goals. In life and in business, too, success is most commonly realised by those who have clearly and concisely predetermined the exact nature of their goals. These individuals are very specific about what they are after. You'll never hear them say anything as vague as 'I'm going to start a business and make lots of money', or 'I hope I play better today.' Such concepts are impossible for the brain to visualise and, since your brain thinks in images, it needs to visualise clearly what it is seeking to achieve. Subconsciously too, such a vague goal is difficult, if not impossible, for the mind to visualise, and therefore hard to focus on and to work towards.

> **First say to yourself what you would be; and then do what you have to do.**
> *Epictetus (AD c. 50 – c. 138), Phrygiam Stoic philosopher*

Your goals may be extremely ambitious, but as long as they're realistic they're achievable.

**To be blind is bad, but it is worse to have eyes and not to see.**
*Helen Keller (1880–1968), American writer*

Bill Gates' clear goal has been to bring personal computers within reach of every householder. Soichiro Honda began his working life as a fifteen-year-old engineering apprentice, but he had already a clearly defined aim, which was to mass-produce cheap motor-cycles in a land which, at the time, depended mainly on horses and bicycles for transport. Mother Teresa's aim was simply to help those who had been abandoned by society. I don't know whether she ever dreamt that the Sisters of Charity would go on to become a worldwide organisation within her own lifetime, but, be that as it may, her goal was very clearly defined.

Have you defined yours?

Every goal starts out as a thought, as a dream: but in the winning mind-set this goal, this image, becomes real, almost tangible – it already exists in the future. When you ask people to describe their perfect house, they can usually draw you an extraordinarily detailed picture. When you ask them to do the same with a car, you get a similar response. But when you ask most people about their life-goal or their perfect future they usually can't tell you so precisely – they haven't clearly defined to themselves what it is they wish to achieve.

Those rare individuals who, by the realisation of their goals, have transformed our lives in the twentieth century not only saw clearly what it was they wanted to achieve, they believed in its attainability. When you ask such people to define success, they usually talk in terms of achievement rather than monetary gain. Financial reward was for them an automatic consequence rather than their main focus.

Whether it's simply to lose a few pounds or to make two extra sales calls a day, or to build up a business that will transform the world, clearly define to yourself whatever it is you wish to achieve.

## Definite plan

'If you fail to plan, then you are planning to fail.' Once you have clearly defined your goal, the next step is to plan exactly how you are going to get there. Furthermore, you need to have faith in your ability to get there, particularly in the case of ambitious goals, which may seem at the outset almost fanciful. You need a plan that you can trust to work even if you don't yet have the evidence to support it. It need not be sophisticated or detailed, or even foolproof – it doesn't have to resemble the blueprints for the Space Shuttle – but what it does need to be is a plan that you can understand and that can give you a starting-point.

It is perfectly all right for your plans to change weekly or even daily, depending on how the situation alters. Indeed, the best plans are infinitely flexible – if they don't work, change them, adapt them – and as often as you need to.

Often in business one comes across plans that are precise and totally rigid. Staff are told: 'This is what is going to happen and this is how we are going to do it.' No individual flair is allowed for, because that would conflict with the nature of the job. But the truth is that if a plan is too inflexible and begins to fail, the whole project will fail; and the goal becomes an even more distant spot on the horizon. The business's confidence in its ability to reach that goal is diminished, and morale slumps.

> **When schemes are laid in advance, it is surprising how often circumstances fit in with them.**
> *Sir William Osler (1849–1919), regius professor of medicine at Oxford University*

In the pursuit of ambitious long-term goals, it is essential to have planned short-term indicators to check whether you are on course. Think of a sailor navigating the ocean or of a pilot flying long distances: they have way points every twenty, fifty and hundred kilometres in some cases, just to confirm that they are on course. So it should be with your plan. Work out the designation. You want to drive from Glasgow to London, say, so you make sure that you know the progress indicators. When you pass by Carlisle, then Manchester and Birmingham, you know you are on track. With life goals, the same principle applies. If you have a long-term aim in mind, make sure you are on track by giving yourself achievable short-term goals. Once one is in the bag, tick the box and move on to the next. Eventually you will see these short-term goals accumulating to create your ultimate goal.

> **Give me a stock clerk with a goal and I'll give you a man who will make history. Give me a man with no goals and I'll give you a stock clerk.**
> *J. C. Penney (1875–1971), American retailer and philanthropist*

When you go shopping, you make a list. You decide in advance what it is you want to buy, knowing that when you get to the shop, you can always take advantage of any special offers, even though they don't figure on your list. But if you don't make a list, it's very easy to arrive home only to discover that you've forgotten something essential. Similarly, if you are going to have a dinner party, you plan who you are inviting and what they are going to eat – you may decide in advance where they are going to sit. You don't leave any of these things to chance because you know they are all important for the success of the evening. Your life is infinitely more important than any dinner party, so don't leave it to chance, either.

If you *don't* plan your personal and professional life-goals, you will be subject to the vagaries of chance and it's quite likely that you'll end up somewhere you don't want to be. Let's say you determine to go to the South Pole. You set off heading south, but it doesn't matter too much if thereafter you sometimes go a tiny bit towards the east or a tiny bit towards the west, because you're still essentially heading south. You are still going in the direction of where you wish to arrive.

In the pursuit of your personal goals you may, of course, be tempted to let someone else map out your route for you – but do this only if you want to end up making *their* journey. Ultimately, you have to plan *your* journey yourself. And remember, when you are clear in your own mind about where you're going, it's best on the whole to keep your plan to yourself. Share it only with those who believe in you.

A famous advert in America for a hamburger chain featured an old hamburger-stall-holder who, opening up a rival's burger, stared inside and said, 'Where's the beef?' Before you take action in pursuit of your dreams, ask yourself, 'Where's the plan?'

## Confidence

The word 'confidence' comes from the Latin *cum* (with) and *fides* (faith): meaning that faith in something or someone – in this case yourself – that comes from the assurance of positive past experience. It's different from arrogance – arrogance is the product of an overinflated ego believing in itself without any evidence to substantiate that belief, and is frequently characteristic of an insecure or *un*confident person. When a company is going through a process of major change, it is very important that the staff are confident that this process will produce an improvement. Once they lose confidence, the change process is severely jeopardised. Confidence is akin to morale; what soldiers always want to know in wartime is what the morale of the enemy is like, because they know that if morale goes so does confidence – and then, invariably, the enemy's chances of victory are slim indeed.

In the business arena, confidence is a very powerful

quality. As Henry Ford said, 'If you think you can or you think you can't, you are usually right.' The capacity of an organisation for strong self-belief gives it the edge over its competitors. People talk of corporate confidence – confident markets, confident trading. We speak of people as being confident in a complimentary manner. Much individual confidence is based on positive experience: the memory of such moments gives us greater self-belief and more faith in our ability to succeed or, at least, to cope with the challenges ahead.

Imagine you've been rushed off to the casualty department of your local hospital. You've had a bit of a bash on your foot, you're in great pain and your ankle needs to be reset. Standing at the door are two doctors, both about the same age. One gives the impression of confidence, the other of arrogance. Who would you want to treat your ankle? I don't know about you, but I'll go for confidence every time. Truly confident individuals and organisations are invariably humble; they have no need to boast of their successes because, having achieved in the past, they have that quiet inner knowledge that they can achieve again. When you're setting an ambitious goal, confidence enables you to rise above the negative values of others, allows you to overcome endless setbacks – even ridicule, fear, hardship and pain. The faith of confident individuals in their ultimate success is critical to the accomplishment of any endeavour. We only have to consider those many famous explorers and scientists whose belief in the achievability of an ambitious future objective was initially met with derision. And confidence inspires others; it is the key component of the leader. Confident companies inspire investors, partners and the market itself. They have experienced success and, critically, they understand their success as an ongoing experience, not necessarily a destination.

But how do we acquire confidence? We can't go to the chemist and buy a bottle of it, but the continual achievement of small personal successes helps us to build it up. In this way our confidence is born not of wishful thinking but of authentic experience, both good and bad; the good reaffirms, and the bad is a lesson not to be repeated. Taking quiet pride in who you are and what you are achieving forms the bedrock upon which your confidence will be built.

> **The great pleasure in life is doing what people say you cannot do.**
> *Walter Bagehot (1826–77), political thinker, economist and literary critic*

## No fear of failure

The future doesn't exist except in our imaginations, though I am sure some science fiction writers might disagree. But although the future doesn't yet exist in any tangible form, we frequently fear it because it is uncertain. Those very imaginations of ours which identify our goals will, in moments of self-doubt, create an equally strong image of failure, something that we shy away from for fear that it will harm us. We tend to see failure as signalling the end of our hopes and wishes, when if we choose to see it positively, it's a new beginning. Think of that child learning to eat and to talk. She doesn't worry about the fact that most of her food ends up almost anywhere but in her mouth when she's feeding herself, nor is she bothered by any grammatical errors she may make when trying to ask her father for her teddy. She isn't influenced by peer group pressure. She is motivated by a natural success mechanism that helps her to achieve, to learn and to survive.

> **Make the most of every failure. Fall forward.**
> *Anon.*

If we use a simple model of fear of failure and look at it

in commercial terms, without oversimplifying the realities of business, we find that the major commercial success stories of the twentieth century, almost without exception, have failed at some point. At some point they risked everything, gambled their future on no more than a whim or a hunch, because they believed implicitly that the rewards of the success that they would achieve would far outweigh the penalties of any failure. Harlan Sanders, the man who founded Kentucky Fried Chicken, consistently failed in his business ventures until the age of sixty-three, when he started marketing his secret formula for a coating for fried chicken. The story goes that the first thousand restaurants he called on said they weren't interested, and he was forced to give his product away, free, in return for a percentage of their chicken sales.

Fear of failure can stop you from even trying, but there really is no great shame in failing. As I said earlier, I believe the greatest shame is in never trying. The point is that no successful person ever associates himself with his failures; he regards them as opportunities to learn valuable lessons. Thomas Edison, a prolific inventor among whose many patents that of the light-bulb was arguably the most renowned, made over seven hundred attempts before finding the right material for the perfect filament. When he was asked how it felt to fail so many times, he replied, 'I haven't failed, I've just found seven hundred ways that didn't work.' He saw it in a positive light (forgive the pun!).

**Godlike genius? Godlike nothing – sticking to it is the genius.**

*Thomas Edison*

Neither our lives nor our careers are races to see who can get there first – they are journeys that produce an equal share of setbacks and of achievements. What matters is your ability to face your fears, to overcome them, and to realise that they only truly exist in your imagination. I'm not suggesting that you now take up cave-diving or bomb disposal as a hobby. Rather, pick one thing that you have always said no to in your life because you were afraid. It could be something as specific as learning to swim, or as general as fear of rejection – or even, fear of success. Examine exactly what it is that you are afraid of, and recognise that fear exists primarily in your mind; that the more you believe in your fear, the more likely it is to become a self-fulfilling prophecy. See your fears for what they are – merely false expectations that appear to be real – and work through them.

Pinned above the desk in my office is a quote: 'At the end of our lives we don't regret the things at which we failed – we regret the things we wished for but never attempted.'

So what are you waiting for?

## Achieving a balance between the four principles

You may ask which of the four essential principles – a clear goal, a definite plan, confidence, or no fear of failure – is the most important. In one way, the goal is the most important because without it you are lost. But equally vital, I think, is banishing the fear of failure, because if you can develop the no-fear mentality you will be able to begin your journey; you will not be the one that fear leaves rooted to the spot, whose projects and plans, brilliant though they may be, remain for ever unrealised.

So balance the four principles carefully. Give priority to a clear goal and to banishing fear. In the creation of a plan, though there is often no obvious route, there is always something you can do to begin the process. The important thing to remember is whatever you do, no matter how simple, it is a beginning. When it comes to the plan, it will probably, once you've devised it, take care of itself; and the little steps you take on the path to success will give you all the confidence you need.

Once you have set your goal, ask yourself three questions:

Where do I want to go?
When do I want to get there?
Why?

**Perhaps it would be a good idea, fantastic as it sounds, to muffle every telephone, stop every motor and halt activity for an hour some day to give people a chance to ponder for a few minutes on what it is all about, why they are living and what they really want.**
*James Truslow Adams (1878–1949), American historian*

The reason for asking these questions is that precisely defining your goal in this way helps to create a clear visual image of it in your subconscious mind. And once you know the where, the when and the why, you will find that the how – How am I going to get there? – often through apparent coincidences and chance events, has, like your plan, a wonderful tendency to take care of itself. You are now fully aware of where you are trying to go, so you will have no difficulty in recognising opportunities when they come your way.

Think again of those times when you've been racking your brains over a problem, and then suddenly out of the blue, while you're having a coffee or just wandering aimlessly along the corridor looking at fire extinguishers, you have that moment of 'That's it!' The solution has suddenly come to you. We read of famous inventors at moments of discovery, or composers scribbling furiously the notes of their new masterpiece. How often have you sat in a meeting, collectively trying to solve a problem, when somebody comes up with an answer and you all immediately recognise it as the right one? Both in corporate and in personal matters, if we just let it get on with the problem, our subconscious decision-making process will get there all on its own.

> **No man ever became great except through many and great mistakes.**
> *William Gladstone (1809–98)*

When I recommend to organisations that they shouldn't worry too much about the 'how' but focus clearly on their aim, I often meet with raised eyebrows if not downright resistance. Of course, ways and means are important, but I can't stress too strongly that clearly defining your goal *must* come first on the list. Then you can work backwards to your plan.

Most successful businessmen and entrepreneurs that I know, when talking about the four principles, confirm my belief that a clear goal is the single most important one. But they usually add that it was a determination to succeed at all costs that drove them on. They also emphasise the role that confidence plays in the selling process and in encouraging those around them, keeping them optimistic during the difficult early stages of any business development programme.

It is vital in all your endeavours to live in the here and now, to take things one day at a time. You must plan for the future, but be flexible enough to change your plan in the confidence that you will eventually arrive at the destination you have set yourself.

## Persistence

I have a vivid memory of myself aged four, sitting on my father's knee in his car one evening in the driveway of our house in Glasgow, listening to *The Goon Show* on the radio. I remember how heartily he was laughing, his whole body shaking – the pleasure he felt was almost tangible. I remember, too, in the days of black and white television, my father letting me stay up to watch a Marx Brothers movie with him. We sat there together, and much of the time he was convulsed with laughter. My father was a physician in Glasgow, before working latterly as a single-handed general practitioner. He died when he was fifty-two, as a result of hard work, stress, and a predisposition to high blood pressure which, being a doctor, he probably chose to ignore. More than anything else from those early times, it is my father's love of laughter that stays with me. On Wednesday afternoons, his half-day, if the weather was wet and it was a school holiday he would take my sisters and me to the cartoon cinema, and we would be almost embarrassed at the volume of his laughter. His favourite of all was Laurel and Hardy. On Saturday mornings he would stop seeing patients at about ten o'clock, then return to the house, which was ten minutes' drive from the surgery. I would be waiting in the lounge for him. Together we would sit down and watch a Laurel and Hardy short. Then, wiping the tears from his eyes, he would get up, drive back to the surgery and start seeing patients again. My father believed in the curative power of laughter; he believed it was good for the body and good for the soul. Certainly, medical studies over the past twenty years seem to confirm that the endorphins that are released into the bloodstream when we laugh create a feeling of well-being.

Like many young boys I grew up wanting to be my father, wanting to be a doctor; alternatively, I rather fancied being a comedian, like Stan Laurel. As I got older I decided that I'd like to be a comedy writer, but I didn't have a clue as to how to go about it. I spoke to a teacher at school who suggested law, and in the end I went to university to study human biology. I wasn't a very academic chap, but I ploughed through as well as I could. Then, at the beginning of my second term, father died very suddenly. I drifted on, uncertain, insecure, and depressed. I was twenty years old, and several hundred miles from home. I was grieving. I drifted at university for another year and a half, then left.

I had begun to realise that the study of human biology was not taking me where I wanted to go, and that I wasn't a very bright student anyway – at least, at that point in my life that's what I believed. A few months earlier I had been to the Edinburgh Festival and seen a student show that had revived my interest in becoming a comedian; in fact I just knew then that this was what I wanted to do. But it wasn't until after leaving university that I took this idea a stage further. For reasons I've never been able to fathom, other than my desperate desire to do it, I went to the Edinburgh Fringe office and asked them how to put on a show. I was told to register, then find a venue. I found an old church hall, which I then sublet to other theatre companies, and in return one let me use their lighting rig, another their staging, another their seating – so now I had a fully equipped theatre in a church hall, and it hadn't cost me a penny.

So with a small group of friends who had happily agreed to get involved, I put on my first show – *The Muff-it Show* (the title was meant to be a sort of parody on *The Muppets*). It was 1978, and after two weeks we had made a profit of £40 which, considering that most shows made a loss, was not bad going. Afterwards I went off to India with a friend, and when I returned I got a 'proper' job, but still in the back of my mind was my desire to be a comedy writer. So in 1980, then again in 1981 and 1982, I went back to the Edinburgh Festival, with the imaginatively named *The Muff-it Show 2, 3* and *4*. On the second day of our fourth Festival we received rave reviews in the *Scotsman* and went on to sell out for twenty-eight consecutive shows, setting a box-office record in the process. We were featured on the radio and appeared on television shows, and were nominated for a Perrier Comedy Award. On the way to a radio studio to give an interview, I met a producer from BBC Radio who asked me if I'd like to write for a show that he was producing in London. More offers followed: all of a sudden, I had become a comedy writer.

**Statistically – 100 per cent of the shots you don't take never go in.**

*Wayne Gretzsky*

The point of this story is that when I dreamt all those years before of wanting to be a comedy writer, although I didn't have a clue as to how to set about it I did have one quality that I now recognise and have since recognised in other successful individuals. Namely, I showed persistence; I didn't quit; I never took my eye off the target.

Someone once told me that Calvin Coolidge, American president during the mid-1920s, was more remembered for the following few wonderful words than for anything he ever did in office:

**Press on. Nothing can take the place of persistence. Talent will not; the world is full of unsuccessful people with talent. Genius will not; unrewarded genius is almost a proverb. Education alone will not; the world is full of educated derelicts. Persistence and determination alone are omnipotent.**

It would be hard to put it more succinctly. In fact, I used to think that maybe persistence was the fifth guiding principle. Now, though, I believe that it's the all-important common thread running through the four principles of success.

Before you start your journey, before you determine exactly how you're going to get to where you want to go, ask yourself this: 'How badly do I want it? How badly do I really want this success?' Because you have to want it so badly that you can see it, smell it, and live it. Unless you can sustain this, you'll lose it. This is a harder process for large organisations than for individuals because, unless the leadership is completely focused, respected, and clear in what it is trying to achieve, the vision will become diluted and confidence eroded. And then, when a crisis arises, in the absence of that steely determination to succeed, chaos will rule.

History is full of people who have persisted. They are frequently the people we call heroes.

All those years ago when I went off to Los Angeles to try my hand at comedy, I spent months going from club to club, trying to get a spot, trying to persuade TV companies to give me a chance to write for them. Along the way, I met a performer whose dream was to become a screenwriter. We became friends. I returned to England, and it was soon afterwards that I was diagnosed with Hodgkin's disease and spent some months in hospital before returning to work in British television. We stayed in touch via the odd letter and phone call, and after a few years he came to visit me. He was no more successful now than he had been when I'd first met him, and one evening, in a moment of concern for his future, I said, 'You've spent four years trying to make it as a screenwriter. You know, maybe it's not your destiny.' And he looked at me and said: 'Hey! I'm going to do it!' 'But what will you do if you never make it?' I asked. His response wj90 as: 'Robin! I'll never know I didn't make it!' So committed was he and so determined to persist until he succeeded that if necessary he would *die* trying; but what he wasn't going to do was quit.

The years passed and the situation remained the same. Then one day I got a phone call: 'Robin, I've just made my first film! I sold a script, they've finished filming it, we're in the edit suite right now! It's happened, and I've just been asked to write another one!' This incident taught me a lesson that I've never forgotten about the individual's ability to persist and endure through repeated failure; about the paramount importance of believing in yourself and never quitting; about getting up again, like the little boy in the poem quoted earlier, every time you fall.

So let's agree to persist in our journey. Let's agree to persevere along the route towards our own personal successes, large or small, whatever they may be. I hope that I'll be able to help you to create and develop a success habit for yourself. Leave those imagined and self-imposed obstacles behind – right now!

**Within you right now is the power to do things you never dreamed possible. This power becomes available to you just as soon as you can change your beliefs.**

*Maxwell Maltz*

# 5   Clear Goals

**The tragedy in life is not in failing to realise one's goals, but in failing to have goals to realise.**

*Isaiah Mayes*

When young children are asked what they want to do when they grow up, they tell you – not for them a mumbled 'I dunno.' They might aspire to being a superhero, or maybe they'll settle for astronaut, but in their mind's eye there's no limit to the range of professions open to them.

**One never goes as far when one doesn't know where one is going.**

*Goethe*

But when they get a bit older, when you ask them what they are going to do when they leave school, they frequently don't know. Ask, and you'll be told 'Something or other' or 'I'll be all right' or 'Just don't worry about it?' And even when we're long past school age, some of us are still talking in these terms.

Think for a moment about the idea of being 'all right' – do you think it's enough? Do you think it's all you deserve, or do you think you deserve more? If you asked a friend who'd been to the cinema, 'How was the film?' and he replied, 'All right', would you want to go and see it? Or would you go to a restaurant reviewed as serving food that was 'all right'? I don't think you would. And the reason is that all right *isn't* all right. In all aspects of your life, as in all aspects of your business, you deserve better than all right. What you should be aiming for is great, fantastic, wonderful. But in order to get beyond the all-right zone, you need to be very clear about where you want to go. Remember, the ability consistently to define goals in clear and succinct terms is a common feature of successful individuals. Ask them what they are trying to do, and they become animated and enthusiastic, describing their goals in a way that leaves you in no doubt about where they are going.

When I worked in television, I often had to present an idea for a show to a commissioning editor or a senior producer – this performance is called 'the pitch'. It's when you present your idea for the first time to a potential buyer, and you get only one chance to do it. For instance, when you pitched a game show, you would describe it in detail, doing your utmost to bring it alive in the buyer's mind, from the host walking on, to the jackpot round, and everything in between. Whatever the format of your show might be, you'd describe it in clear visual terms – that's because we think in visual terms, in images. When people pitch a movie, they don't say, 'Oh, it's a film about science fiction and there's going to be some special-effects action and some romance', and leave it at that. They describe in great detail both the story and what the film is going to look like on the screen.

It's the same with both *professional* and *personal* goals. Be under no misapprehension: an objective that isn't clearly defined will lack substance and will have only an indistinct reality in your mind. (So it's no surprise that it won't impress itself on anyone else, either.)

This lack of a firm objective is the number one reason for uncertainty. Uncertainty in turn creates, at a personal level, feelings ranging from complacency and boredom to insecurity and even pervasive anxiety. Similarly in the business context, companies that show a lack of certainty about the future create an environment of mistrust, and the workforce becomes demoralised. If a company doesn't know where it's going, it's more than likely that it's going nowhere; and going nowhere is not much to look forward to.

I remember seventeen years ago standing on a street in an Edinburgh suburb called Morningside, waiting for someone to bring the keys to let me into a house I had rented. As I stood there, two old ladies walked slowly past. One said to the other, 'It's important to have something to look forward to.' Her friend agreed: 'Oh yes, so important.' Those words have stayed with me, because if we don't have something in the future to aim at we become uncertain, we feel insecure, and the future becomes a frighteningly empty place.

Do be sure that any personal goals you pursue are yours and not ones that someone else has set for you, for of those you have no ownership. By contrast, in business, of course, group ownership and collective agreement are essential.

Start by asking yourself, 'What am I doing with my life?' How often have you put this question to yourself? I mean how often have you really sat down and worked at it until you've come up with an honest answer? Very rarely, if at all, probably. People say they are too busy just keeping their heads above water . . . the pace of modern life makes it difficult to aim at anything more ambitious than survival. But ignore those doubts, and ask yourself what you are doing with your life at this moment, and where you want it to go. We all want to be accomplished, respected, successful; we want to be admired for our achievements yet we seem to spend so much time running around and *not* doing the most important thing we can do with our time – just sitting down and thinking about what it is we want to do. We could make a start simply by converting our worrying time into thinking time.

The good use and the misuse of time and energy are well contrasted in the little story of the two people in the swimming pool, both expending the same amount of energy and splashing lots of water about. But while one is purposefully swimming length after length, the other is in the process of drowning.

Are you swimming or drowning? It is so important that you use your energy constructively in setting and achieving your goals. It goes without saying that your goals should always be ultimately for good – for the good of yourself, your family, your company, your society, for the world around you. But the most important thing of all if you're going to achieve your goals is – that's right! – to make sure they are clearly defined.

## Where do you want to go?

Imagine jumping into a taxi and telling the driver, 'Quick! Somewhere!' (Try it sometime on the way home, and see what happens.) The taxi driver, obviously, would be utterly perplexed. I am amazed how many people, when asked where they want to go, reply, 'I want to make a lot of money', 'I want freedom', 'I want to be successful', 'I want to be happy.' (Do any of these sound familiar?) What's happening here is that they are confusing worthwhile desires, aspirations, with defined goals. And though I do believe that success is not a fixed destination but rather an experience along the way, we must have a focal point.

But we need to choose that focal point carefully. In a competitive business environment companies often find themselves focusing on short-term survival – on the next quarter or the next six months. This means that long-term goals are sacrificed, or lost sight of, or simply never formulated. And the penalties of this can be high. In the early 1900s, after over one hundred and fifty years of trading, one of the oldest companies in America, a manufacturer of horse-drawn buggies, finally closed its doors. It had gone out of business because, with the rise in automobile production, people no longer wanted horse-drawn buggies.

Years later a commentator used this firm as an example of a business that became obsolete through its inability to identify other opportunities. Their problem was that they believed they were in the buggy business. What they should have understood was that they were in the transportation business. Instead of focusing on changing the product they set themselves the goal of surviving, and in so doing buried their heads in the sand – to fatal effect.

By contrast, some of the companies that are now giants in their field, great corporations such as Komatsu, Canon and Honda, got there by setting themselves twenty- and thirty-year goals. They focused on a point way ahead in the future and said, 'This is what we want to achieve by that date. This is where we want to go.' In Japan Matsushita, a major holdings company with extensive business interests, has a three-hundred-year strategic plan. This may sound crazy, but it helps them in their decision-making process by continually posing the question: are today's investments going to help future generations achieve the long-term objective?

I remember an American college football team which, though it had never been particularly successful, became very focused and motivated on reaching the national finals. Throughout the season they played like lions and, against all the odds, they got to the final, only to be very heavily defeated. When asked afterwards why they lost, their coach replied, 'Because winning wasn't our goal – unfortunately, we made our goal reaching the final. Next time it'll be to win the championship.'

At a personal level, being very clear about what it is we want to achieve has a major impact on our ability to be successful. When we are young we have many ambitions, but as we get older we tend to lose sight of them, mainly because of difficult life situations. Our young dreams fade; we believe they are now unrealisable. What happens as a result of this is that we never see things through. But there *is* a way of overcoming it. Simply resolve never to stop seeing yourself as achieving those early ambitions.

**What you think of yourself is much more
important than what others think of you.**

*Seneca*

To do this, we have to project and visualise a future
scenario where we have already realised success. We
must be determined not to allow ourselves to get trapped
in our current situation just because we can't resist the
sense of safety, the feeling of cosiness, it gives us. We
must not become rooted to the spot because it's just too
difficult, too risky, to do anything else.

So make the effort now, and get outside your comfort
zone. How far outside is up to you. But like the bird
trapped in the cage, when the door is opened you must
find the courage, the belief in yourself, to embark on a
journey that you will not give up until you've arrived.

Think of our heroes, think of those brave souls who set
out, often without maps, to discover uncharted land
masses, knowing that there was a new world to be found.
You need to experience that same level of belief and
excitement at the journey that awaits *you*. Some of *your*
route may take you into uncharted territory: see it as the
adventure that it is, and embrace it.

## How badly do you want it?

A young pilgrim was sitting by a riverside with his
master. He told the master that for many years he had
meditated and sought illumination in order to discover
God, but he had never come close to enlightenment.
'What must I do to find God?' he asked the master. The
master looked at the young man, then pushed his head
under the water and held it there for some time. After
frantically struggling for several moments against the
hands that held him down, with all the strength he could
muster the young man broke free of the master's grip, got
his head above the water and started to gasp for breath.

'Why did you do that to me?' he spluttered, to which the master replied, 'When your desire for enlightenment is as great as your desire for that breath, then you will be ready.'

The story is told in a spiritual context but its appropriateness to *your* situation is very clear – you must want to achieve your goal as badly as a drowning man seeks air. You must be absolutely committed, in your heart and mind, to the goal you have set yourself. We're talking about your life here – how seriously do you take it? If you're thinking of just dabbling, of having a go for a bit and seeing what happens – don't bother – because it won't work.

Why do you want to achieve this goal? What are the benefits that it will bring you? You have to understand what those benefits are, because they are your spur to success and will keep you going through the bad times.

Think of all those people that we see running the marathon in London and New York. Often they are slightly disabled or elderly, a bit overweight, people who have determined to complete the twenty-six miles and 385 yards in their own time – however long it takes. Not for them the two and a quarter hours of the gold-medallist – they'll have to keep going for four, five, even seven hours. But they all have one thing in common: they're all going to cross that line. Gold-medallist and pensioner alike, and everyone else as well – all are determined to make it, determined not to quit. And the reward and the sense of achievement they gain will be satisfaction enough, something they will treasure for the rest of their lives.

I've mentioned before how important it is, when you set out to achieve a purely personal goal, not to share it with anyone who's likely to pour scorn on it. People who regale you with their negative opinions may well devalue your ambition in your own eyes or, at worst, they will simply destroy your dream. Their reasons for doing this are many, but most often they are afraid of being left behind. They may be jealous of your potential success, for that will only highlight their own sense of failure. So do not share your goals with anyone who will do anything other than support you, encourage you, share your dream and look forward with you to its realisation. This same person can be your personal coach, who, when you trip once too often, will help you to pick yourself up and encourage you to never say die.

Set your goal not only in your mind, but also in your heart. Goals that live only in the mind, without emotional commitment, often become little more than wishes that, through distractions or changes in our circumstances, we have allowed to atrophy. For true success, you need to feel a desire to reach your goal that is so great that it occupies both your head and your heart. When this happens, you will have created passion with purpose, and there is no more winning combination than that.

Goran Kropp of Stockholm conceived the idea, back in 1991, of travelling overland to Nepal under his own steam and then, entirely without back-up, of climbing Mount Everest without oxygen, then returning home the same way. His goal was ambitious, certainly; realistic, possibly. First, he did a feasibility study which involved driving the route, then set about raising the £200,000 sponsorship the trip would cost. He started his physical training with the Swedish cross-country skiing team, in order to build up his cardiovascular capacity. On a specially built bike he set out on 16 October 1995, and since it was a totally un-supported expedition he had to carry all his equipment, which weighed a staggering 129 kilos.

After four months and six days he arrived at Kathmandu, from where he set about moving his equip-ment towards the base camp; the seventy-three kilo load could be moved only fifty metres at a time, with a ten-minute rest in between. For the first time he began to seriously doubt his ability to achieve his objective. The effort needed, he said, afforded him the single most gruelling physical experience of his life.

He made the summit on his third attempt, then came back down the mountain, got on his bike and cycled the twelve thousand kilometres back to Sweden. One year and eight days after leaving he reached home.

Our goals inspire us, and they inspire others. We feel the enthusiasm and passion that *they* generate, and this in turn gives us confidence. Let us be worthy of our goals, and proud of them. Let them be of real benefit – to ourselves, to those around us and to society in general.

> **We make a living by what we get, we make a life by what we give.**
> *Sir Winston Churchill (1874–1965)*

But you must want to achieve that goal so badly that neither your passion nor your purpose ever wavers; so that they see you through those times when neither your target seems unreachable or you feel like giving up. At those times, it is your passion and your purpose that will keep you on track.

## Define exactly

We have discussed the necessity of creating a detailed mental picture of your goal, but seeing it mentally is not enough. To prevent that picture from becoming fuzzy round the edges, you must also write your goal down. Writing something down contributes to the process of helping your subconscious mind to form a clear picture of exactly what it is you are doing, because the very process of writing creates a much more forceful image and generates a more powerful future memory.

However great your ability and concentration, just like the archer, if you have no target to aim at, you will be unable to demonstrate that ability. The physical action of writing and returning daily to the clearly defined goals that you have set reinforces your subconscious vision.

The more powerfully you imagine your goal, the more effectively your subconscious mind will be able to move towards it.

## See it in your mind's eye

Visualisation is the active engaging of your imagination in order to create a picture of a future desired situation. In other words, it's a scripted daydream. If you have ever daydreamed, you're capable of active visualisation. You may have come across the concept before – perhaps in the context of health care, helping patients to 'see' themselves well again; or in the gym or sports arena, where athletes use it to 'see' themselves winning. I know of salesmen who visualise successful meetings before they enter the conference room – they find this gives them almost a sense of familiarity when they begin their sales pitch.

At Yale University in the 1950s a questionnaire was sent out to fifteen hundred students; the topics ranged from the quality of food in the canteen to the accessibility of the library. It's the last two questions that are interesting here: 'Do you have an ambition for your life?' and 'Have you written it down?' Twenty-five years later, a postgraduate who came across this questionnaire was interested enough in these two questions to do a bit of further research. He discovered that over 75 per cent of the fifteen hundred had had an ambition for their life, but only 3.3 per cent had written it down. He tracked down as many of them as he could, and found that every one of the fifty-one students who had written their goals down, all those years ago had gone on to realise their personal dreams – in commerce, in government, and in the professions. The others told him that most of what they'd achieved had happened more by chance than by design; they'd mostly ended up in careers they hadn't planned for because they hadn't defined exactly what it was they were seeking to do.

I believe that writing your goal down is so effective because it actively programs or reprograms your brain to an objective; it actively changes the way you subconsciously perceive. You may have seen the effect that a stage hypnotist can produce by putting people into a trance, and then, at a subconscious level, instructing them to do things. Though it's not a method of self-hypnosis, writing things down helps to ingrain the goal in your subconscious mind and, once the information is there, the subconscious works continuously to make it a reality.

The brain reinforces its images not just with visual signals, but also with sound, smell and other sensory signals, and the act of writing something down serves as a physical reinforcement. Your wonderful brain, in all its complexity, now sets about achieving the task that you have set it – working non-stop, until it realises its goal, of making your vision a reality.

## Ideas are currency

I do not believe that there is such a thing as a bad idea – an idea is simply an idea. It may be appropriate, it may be inappropriate, but ultimately the task in hand will determine which. Every goal, every dream we have, starts off as a thought, so the more creative our thoughts, the more ambitious our dreams, the more opportunities we are creating for ourselves. When we have a clearly defined goal in our minds that we revisit daily, both by writing it down and by visualising it, our subconscious mind works non-stop to reinforce that image. Often we are afraid to think big because we fear ridicule, or believe that our goal is too ambitious. Don't be afraid. Think big, start small.

The most remarkable ability that we have, the one that sets us apart from other species, is our ability to harness our imagination. It is imagination that has allowed us to overcome huge difficulties, to create great art and entertainment, to discover cures for countless ills, and to dream of things unseen and unmade and make them a reality. If you are asked what your goal is by someone you know you can safely confide it to, make sure you have an answer: you should have so much to say that you'll fear taking up too much of that person's time.

> **Formulate and indelibly stamp on your mind a mental picture of yourself as succeeding. Hold this picture tenaciously. Never permit it to fade – and your mind will seek to develop the picture.**
> *Norman Vincent Peale (1898–1993), positive thinking guru*

As children we are read stories about wizards and fairies and genies who will grant us three wishes; and as we grow older, we still occasionally wonder what we would wish for if we had those three wishes. I have never encountered anyone who could not tell me what theirs would be, whether practical or fanciful. So apply your mind to it now and set yourself three life wishes. Then stop wishing, and make them your life goals. A wish is simply a dream you hope for but don't believe in; a goal is a tangible reality you do believe in.

We hear a lot, in business, about the shared ownership of business planning. When individuals are able to input their creative suggestions within organisations, new possibilities are opened up. The essential point is that everyone has the ability to come up with an idea that could change the way a job is done, or find the solution to an old problem. And yet all too frequently people will dismiss an idea out of hand because of its source.

I have often seen ideas belittled and ridiculed in business, and working in television I saw the same – it's the worst thing anyone can ever do. Apart from the fact that you are undermining somebody's self-confidence, you are destroying a very viable asset – a potential source of future ideas. The person we think of as not very bright may one day come out with that pearl of wisdom that will save all our lives or change the way we do things for ever.

It is important to understand in a brainstorming business situation that opinions are simply opinions – they are not facts. Recognise the difference. When putting a plan together, look at as many options as possible and then discuss them in a professional and respectful manner – don't belittle anyone's contribution. Point out in a friendly way that a particular idea doesn't fit in with the objective, if that's what you think, and if the originator of the idea cannot defend it move on to the next.

In 1990 Toyota employed forty-seven thousand people in Japan, who in that year generated a staggering 1.8 million suggestions. I think we can take it that those employees felt involved and appreciated. I have no doubt that their shared ownership of the company and of its manufacturing process had a great deal to do with this. And it would go some way towards explaining how they created the Lexus, a luxury car that went in record time from drawing-board to showroom, then to a prime position in the highly competitive luxury car market.

> **Good business leaders create a vision, articulate the vision, passionately own the vision, and relentlessly drive it to completion.**
> *Jack Welch, (1935– ), chairman and chief executive officer of General Electric*

When you brainstorm, try not to put a short time-frame on the process. In business situations I write the problem on a large sheet of paper on a wall – or flip-chart, and during the following week anyone can come along and write suggestions on it, adding more paper if needed. In this way the brain is allowed to work on the solution for one to five days. It's astonishing how often what comes up after day 4 bears no relationship to what was thought of on day 1.

Shortly before his death Albert Einstein admitted: 'I

know quite certainly that I myself have no special talent. Curiosity, obsession and dogged endurance combined with self-criticism have brought me my ideas.' Whatever business you are in, think of yourself as being first and foremost in the ideas business. So encourage, nurture and develop those ideas; otherwise, you will be taking a step back before you have begun.

## Guaranteed success

As the American evangelist Dr Robert Schuller famously asked, What would you attempt if you knew you could not fail? What would you wish for one year from today if success was absolutely guaranteed? And knowing that success was guaranteed, how confident would you feel as you approached your target? With what degree of confidence, and with what kind of attitude, would you tackle setbacks and difficulties? How committed, how determined, how passionate would you be?

I believe that success *is* guaranteed if we pursue our goals with one hundred per cent belief in their achievability; if we understand that success at a personal level is the gradual realisation of our individual goals, then small incremental steps towards our goals are successes too, and each step we take that brings us closer to our long-term life goals is a step successfully taken.

As I said earlier, the pursuit of our goals at a personal level is a solo journey. But in a business it is a shared one – which can often make the experience less worrying, because there are always others there to encourage us at times when confidence is low. And I believe that because success is not a one-stop destination but an ongoing experience on our journey into the future, we must continually be setting ourselves new goals as we achieve those we set earlier. The often spontaneous little successes that we achieve en route are part of the process, and as long as we commit ourselves to the journey and never give up we will experience the ultimate success.

Only you can know whether your personal success is a true reflection of the commitment you have invested in achieving it.

> **This above all: to thine own self be true,**
> **And it must follow, as the night the day,**
> **Thou canst not then be false to any man.**
> *William Shakespeare (1564–1616); Hamlet, Act III,*
> *scene 2*

You can fool those around you – at work it is possible to fake commitment or enthusiasm – but you cannot kid yourself. You cannot fake your own passion for success. As long as you are working towards your goals with as much passion and commitment as you can muster, you are on your way.

It's a sad fact that many people have the same commitment to failing as successful individuals have to succeeding.

Of course, if we choose to we can carry our failures and setbacks around with us for the rest of our lives like unwanted luggage; we can continue to use them as excuses, as stumbling-blocks, as something to fall back on whenever we are faced with a challenge. In this way we use them to create our self-image – one of failure – which can only create failure in the future and will ultimately stop us from even trying.

I can't emphasise enough how important it is, when you look back on your past, to remember your successes, no matter how small. Leave your unwanted baggage behind; shed your negative experiences and your negative self-image; don't identify with your failures.

When I was first exposed to this concept I thought it was almost delusory in its simplicity, but when I examined my life I realised that every failure I had encountered was one I had expected and unwittingly pre-determined. A minority of people have an exceptionally deep-rooted failure habit; if this is our particular problem, we can seek professional assistance to overcome it with the help of a counsellor or therapist. But one basic thing that we can all do is to promise ourselves never to quit, and when that becomes our core determination, our success is guaranteed.

## Dare to dream

As I said earlier, nothing was ever created that did not first exist as a dream in someone's imagination. No matter how fantastic, it existed clearly in the mind of the person who imagined it. So what's stopping you, or your business, from thinking big?

If you look at the largest organisations in the world today, you can trace their origins back to an individual or a small group of people who came together with a common dream. However small they were when they started out, they had great hopes for the future, great plans for the company. And, just as I was advised to when I first went into business many years ago, they were 'thinking big, starting small'.

> **I am one, but I am only one. I cannot do everything; but I will not let what I cannot do interfere with what I can do.**
> *Edward Everett Hale (1822–1901), American writer and Unitarian clergyman*

Belief in the dream is everything – otherwise, you predetermine failure. And don't just pay lip-service to that dream: if you don't have absolute faith in it, you'll undermine it completely. It will be like building a house with no foundations. Have you ever heard someone say, 'Well, I hope for the best but I'm prepared for the worst', 'Things never work out for me, but I'll give it a go.' What they don't realise when they say this is that they are predetermining their failure – they have created in their own mind the belief that their goal is bound to elude them.

Winners are the people who don't find excuses. They don't procrastinate, they don't go around saying, 'Oh, I can't do that because . . .' They have dropped all their unwanted baggage and are focusing clearly on creating the future.

So what's holding *you* back? Sit down and concentrate on what it is that you would love to happen in your life, no matter how improbable it might appear to other people, and then give it a reality check – is this an achievable goal? Think of it this way: if you aim for the stars and come up short, you still might make it to the moon. Which means at the very least that you will have taken yourself from where you are further towards where you want to be. As the saying goes: when you really want to do something you'll find a way – and when you don't you'll find an excuse.

George Foreman, the former heavyweight boxing champion of the world, once said, 'If you don't dream, you might as well be dead.' I think that what he meant was that it is our dreams that give us hope, our dreams that give us, as the old lady I overheard in Edinburgh say, 'something to look forward to'. So dream big, start small. And start now.

People frequently mistake the limits of their own vision for the limits of the world.

## Starting out

When is the best time to start our journey towards those goals that we have now clearly defined? Now – if not physically, then mentally. Starting any journey or endeavour requires us to act – confidently and promptly – to stop us from hesitating. If we hesitate, we may put things off for weeks, for months, even for ever, and finish up like those old people who, when asked what they would do differently if they had their time again, offer such movingly simple things: just to walk barefoot on the beach, or to tell a certain person at a certain time that they loved them, or to change jobs, or to try to set up their own business, or to travel more. These things that we may take for granted are chances they didn't take.

*Your* chance is now. Every day can be a fresh start if you want it to be, so don't look for reasons not to get on with it. Don't say you're going to start your diet, give up smoking, or think about asking your bank manager for a loan in the near future. Do it now.

New Year's resolutions are almost always self-defeating. You may have noticed that if you habitually decide on 1 January that you will stop whatever it may be, or start whatever it may be, you generally manage to keep it up until approximately the 3rd or 4th of the month. Inevitably, your brain draws upon the memory of previous failures, so when you determine, as we all have at some time or other, to get up forty minutes earlier and go for a run, you may stick at it for two or three weeks, but your memory of never succeeding will allow you to justify your failure because 'that's just the way it's always been'.

There's a particular aspect of your life or your business that you'd like to be different? Then start immediately, mentally if not physically, to prepare yourself for change. You cannot discover new oceans until you have courage to lose sight of the shore.

Write down all the reasons why you should start now, list all the potential benefits to yourself – this in itself will strengthen your resolve. And as your self-esteem increases from your small successes along the way, so the journey will become more meaningful, the process more exciting, and you will become more enthusiastic, more confident – and happier. The effects are external as well as internal: you'll find that people notice this new confidence, this inner knowledge that comes from clearly knowing where you are going. It's not arrogance, either.

You *know* you are going to get there. So begin today. Commit yourself to losing that excess weight, to going for that promotion, to rewriting your CV, to sorting out your relationship with your boss.

Live that dream. All it takes is a clearly defined goal that is in keeping with your core values and that you are passionately committed to. As the advert says, 'Do it now!' because you won't want to look back twenty or thirty years from now, wishing you had this chance again.

You have it now – so take it!

# 6 Plan, Plan, Plan

Walking one evening in Amsterdam after a business meeting, a Dutch colleague and I passed a chess café; all the tables had boards on them, and many intelligent-looking people were pondering their games. My friend asked if I would like a game. Never being one to turn down a challenge, I replied, 'Certainly.' When he asked me if I was a good player I told him, jokingly, that I was not just good but excellent (though I think my note of irony got lost in translation). So we sat down, duly ordered two beers, laid out the chessboard and commenced battle. I played quickly and in a random manner. Martin, on the other hand, pondered long over almost every move, studied the board, looked at me, looked at the board again, then carefully made his reply. After six or seven minutes he looked me in the eye and said in exasperation, 'You don't have a strategy, do you?' Somewhat sheepishly I admitted as much. 'No wonder I can't work out what you're doing,' he said. 'It's chaotic.' A few moves later, checkmate to him.

In the absence of a plan we have chaos, pure and simple: there's no other way of describing it. Martin had been a chess champion at the age of seventeen; it was inconceivable to him that anyone should play without a strategy, because there are too many variations in chess for victory ever to be left to chance. As we played, he said, he was looking for *my* strategy – hence his perplexity.

In this chapter we will look at the whole issue of strategy: its creation, application and adaptation.

Whenever you buy something, be it a washing-machine, a VCR, or especially a piece of self-assembly furniture, it always comes with instructions. They may, as we often joke, be incomprehensible, but my point is that the manufacturers know that they must supply a plan, a pattern of instruction, to guide us towards the desired outcome.

Planning is as natural to the process of success as its absence is to the process of failure.

Think of the Space Shuttle, an extraordinarily complex machine with tolerances of operation beyond any machine ever constructed. Needless to say, none of its development will have been left to anything resembling my chess-playing style. Every part of its design and construction was planned in detail; the exact specification of each component was designed, built, tested and redesigned as often as necessary, until they got it right. In a sense, the building of the Space Shuttle is not so different from making that first bookshelf: first you determine what sort of bookshelf it's going to be, and then you plan a strategy to achieve it. Of course, it's not as complex as building the Space Shuttle (though at times it may feel like it).

Keep your plan simple, because the more parts it has, the more links you are putting into its chain and the chain is only as strong as its weakest link. The more points of reference you build in that will allow you to measure progress towards your goal, the better.

When devising your plan, there are two simple questions that you need to answer: where do you want to go, and when do you want to arrive there? Answering these questions about the destination and the time-frame helps you to plan the 'how' process.

**There is a giant asleep within every man.**
**When the giant awakes, miracles happen.**
> *Frederick Faust (1892–1944), aka Max Brand,*
> *American screenwriter*

I hope I've already convinced you that, when you set out to achieve a goal, whether personal or professional, it's very important that you write down your plan. Creating a blueprint for success becomes a powerfully remembered instruction to yourself. The written plan is a guide to which you can return daily, then examine your progress and, if necessary, adapt your procedure accordingly. When you hold a plan only vaguely in your mind, when it's something you occasionally think about but have not articulated well to yourself – or written down, the reference points become unclear and your progress towards your goal is hampered.

As I said earlier, any plan must allow for flexibility. As a chess game progresses, so the players may need to change their strategy. And along with flexibility goes personal commitment: a plan is only as effective as your commitment to following it through.

Let's take an example. Suppose you have identified a very clear goal and believe it to be realistic and achievable. You are prepared to do what it takes and are fully committed to giving it your absolute best. You have decided you would like to be a travel writer.

Where do you start? You start by asking yourself some questions: What skills will I have to acquire? Will I need to improve my writing ability? How will I go about getting my work published? Is there anyone who can help me with any of this?

In finding the answers to these questions you begin to acquire the knowledge that you need in order to start creating your plan. You will first have written down your goal – you want to become a travel writer. Then break that down into a number of smaller goals to be achieved en route. The first goal could be to improve your writing to a level where you are confident enough to begin submitting articles. To do this you may need to join creative-writing night classes or a writing group. If you think your style isn't descriptive enough, go and see an English tutor or a published author and ask them if they can help you. In the early planning stages you will often find that much of the information and assistance is freely available. Advice is free. Make sure to write these interim goals down too, so you can return to them every day and check your progress; and if any part of your plan is not working, examine why and change it.

> **There is only the moment. The now. Only what you are experiencing at this second is real. This does not mean you live for the moment. It means you live *in* the moment.**
>
> *Leo Buscaglia*

Constructing a plan looks easy in theory: in practice, there will be setbacks, discouragements and upsets along the way – rejection letters, for instance, or the ridicule of a friend you thought would be supportive. The kind and seriousness of the obstacles you encounter will vary in proportion to the ambitiousness of the goal, which is why your complete commitment and self-belief are so important. Occasionally you will come up against an obstacle so great that you genuinely believe you can't overcome it. But there is no obstacle you cannot overcome if you are sufficiently determined. There is always a way – often it does not appear obvious, but there *is* always a way.

If you really get stuck, look at how others have dealt with similar setbacks. You'll never be the first person to have encountered this particular problem. Military strategists, corporate strategists, chess players studying the strategies of past Grand Masters – all of them know that finding out and learning from what others have done in similar situations is a prerequisite of success.

Do the same. Study the strategies used by those who have accomplished what you are seeking to achieve. Learn from their experiences and be inspired by them. Whatever worked for them, whatever made them successful, may well work for you. Make the study of other people's approaches part of your plan.

# Learn from your mistakes

I said earlier that if your plan is not working, change it. Having a flexible plan means that you are *willing* to change it. The important thing is to be able to learn from your mistakes. So often people don't: they repeat the same mistakes and end up with the same result.

There was a Russian Intelligence officer during the Cold War, who arrived one day at his friend's house with both ears heavily bandaged. 'What happened?' his friend exclaimed. The officer replied, 'I was ironing my shirt when suddenly the phone rang, and without thinking I stuck the iron against my ear!' And his friend said, 'But what happened to the other ear?' 'Oh, I did that when I phoned for the ambulance!' he answered. Sometimes we get so locked in to one way of doing something, one way of thinking, that we believe it impossible to find an alternative solution.

I also rather like the story of the wise old monk who, every morning before dawn, went to the temple to pray. Every day as he began his prayers, the temple cat would walk in and brush up against him and distract him. Eventually he decided to take some string into the temple and tie the cat to the altar while he said his devotions. This continued every day for many years until the old monk died. Then the young monks continued the tradition of tying the cat to the altar every morning during their devotions. One day the cat died, so they got another one. After another hundred years of cats being tied to the altar, somebody said, 'This is silly – why don't we get a statue?' So they got a statue and put it at the bottom of the altar, and after another hundred years another monk said, 'This is such a beautiful statue, it's so old, it's such a wonderful tradition – I think we should put it on top of the altar.' And so as the years went by the monks used to sit and worship this cat, and no one ever really knew why they did it, but it had always been there, so there had to be a reason.

Too often, we just accept the way we do things, without thinking. But don't be afraid to challenge your goals; don't be afraid to challenge your plans; don't be afraid to challenge yourself. When companies tell me that they do things in a certain way because that's the way they've always done them and they don't want to change their working practices just for the sake of changing them, I always agree with their viewpoint. Changing things for no reason is pointless. But the fact is that if there is any constant in our lives – especially our business life – it is change itself. Change is the one thing that we encounter continually. And since in order to survive businesses must continually evolve, so the process of adaptation and change should come naturally to them. A natural evolution. Today's giants will become to-morrow's dinosaurs unless they respond to the need for change.

If your plan is rigid, if it cannot bend, it will snap. This is why it must be flexible. If the time-frame you originally conceived proves too short, then extend it, reset the date. If, on the other hand, you are ahead of schedule, don't worry about bringing your plan forward – it's your business, no one else's. If you allow yourself the flexibility to change your blueprint as you go along, you won't be demoralised by changes when they occur. Often the goals we set ourselves are moving targets and so we actually *need* a moving plan – and I don't mean one that makes us cry when we look at it.

*Rules for being human*
**You will learn lessons.**
**There are no mistakes – only lessons.**
**A lesson is repeated until it is learned.**
**If you don't learn lessons, they get harder (pain is one way the universe gets your attention).**
**You'll know you've learned a lesson when your actions change.**

*Anon.*

# Ask for help (when you need it)

Casanova lay on his deathbed. Suddenly, there was a knock at the front door and a young man appeared: 'I must speak to Casanova, for only he has the knowledge to answer my question. It is essential that I speak to him.' Casanova's doctor replied, 'That's not possible, because he is gravely ill and cannot see anyone apart from his close family.' On hearing the noise outside Casanova asked that the visitor be let in. So the young man went in and knelt at Casanova's bedside and said, 'Casanova, you have made love to over twelve hundred of the most beautiful women in Italy.' Casanova looked at him and said, 'Fifteen hundred!' 'All right, all right, fifteen hundred of the most beautiful women in Italy. But how did you do it?' Casanova beckoned him to lean closer, and whispered in his ear: 'I asked.'

How often in your own life have you failed to ask for help? How often do you complain about things that don't seem fair – promotions that have passed you by, opportunities that have not been freely available to you? Yet in most circumstances all you had to do was to ask.

When creating your plan, do ask for information, for advice, for the help you require. Twenty minutes with an expert or with somebody who has achieved what you are attempting will be invaluable. It will be time well spent. If you were walking along the roadside and a car pulled over and the driver asked you for directions, would you help him? I believe most people would. Isn't it interesting that when strangers come and ask us for help, we listen to their requests and, if we *can* assist them, we will? This is such an invaluable resource: never overlook it. At work, if you want to learn a skill, talk to somebody who has it: benefit from their shared knowledge and experience. And when you've gained the knowledge you want, respect it. It will be an asset that will help to reinforce your vision. Knowledge is power, it's said. But knowledge without action is simply knowledge. So act upon the knowledge that you glean.

If you had the chance to go back in your life and ask one person a question, who would it be and what would you ask them? Now determine never to miss such an opportunity again.

When I was being treated for Hodgkin's, the professor asked to see me one day when I went for a routine check-up. I figured this was definitely bad news because I had never been asked to see such a senior member of staff before: obviously my sell-by date was up. I went into his examination room. 'How are you?' he asked. Now, I wasn't sure if this was a leading question so I kind of hedged my bets and said, 'Pretty good.' Then he told me why I'd been summoned. With the amount of clinical research he did, he explained, he rarely got a chance to see out-patients, and he'd asked reception to send him some that day. My name had come out of the lucky dip. Then he asked if I had any questions – and boy oh boy, did I!

I asked him everything – from things I had read about the latest scientific research, to home-made recipes for curing people of the disease. After we'd talked, he told me to write down any further questions I might have, for next time. So two months later when I went back for a check-up, I pulled out my thick notepad. And did he earn his money that day! Later I was asked to speak to some young people with Hodgkin's, to share my experience with them from the patient's perspective, to answer their questions about the experience, the treatment and the likely emotional reactions they might expect to have. I think I became something of a mentor to them: somebody they could ask questions of, somebody who would listen, offer encouragement, help set strategies, and keep them focused and positive. Anyway, this is what I tried to do for them and it's what a mentor should do for you if you can find one – someone you trust and who will share their experiences with you.

I once read that 48 per cent of those who ask for a pay

rise actually get one. I mentioned this at a lecture one day and somebody said, 'Yes, but fifty-two per cent don't!' Talk about negative thinking! I replied that those 52 per cent were no worse off than they had been before they asked, but the point was lost. Asking for help, for guidance, for encouragement, is your responsibility and yours alone. You can't *expect* others to come up and offer you the job or the pay rise you want, unless you first make it known to them that this is what you are after. Your friends, your family, your colleagues, your associates – even strangers – will help you if you ask. They will give you that essential guidance and encouragement that everyone needs on their journey to success.

> **Go out on a limb – that's where the fruit is.**
> *Will Rogers (1879–1935), American humorist and*
> *stage, film and radio actor*

## Contingency plans

It is important, when you plan, to devise a contingency, a back-up plan, an alternative that you can put in place if something fails to go according to expectations. When the SAS put a plan together, it's a collective process: if four men are going on an exercise, then they all share ownership of the planning. And that planning always involves the critical question: 'What if . . .?' What if the car breaks down? What if we lose the satellite navigation equipment? What if the helicopter doesn't make the rendezvous? For each and every eventuality they have a contingency plan – which is essential, because it gives them both the practical options that will allow them to complete their objective, and the greater confidence that *knowing* they have those alternative options brings with it.

Your goal in life may promise little of the drama of an SAS mission, but I know that it is equally important to you that you succeed. So do make sure you have a back-up plan. Ask yourself, 'What's the worst thing that could happen?' Then imagine it happening, and say to yourself, with commitment, passion and self-belief, 'So what? I can overcome that! If necessary, I can start again!' And so you can if you have anticipated the problem and provided yourself with a solution.

**Never mistake a single defeat for final defeat.**
*F. Scott Fitzgerald (1896–1940), American novelist*

It never ceases to amaze me, when I'm engaged in a creative exercise with a group of people, how truly creative they can be. When running a management seminar for sixty executives from a large company, I gave them this brief: 'Imagine that in a year's time you could achieve every goal you want to achieve for your company. Define what it is you would like to achieve one year from today, identify all the obstacles you might face on your journey to that future point, then present to the rest of the group solutions to those problems.' One hour later, each member of the group presented his own vision of his company's future, then identified the problems and offered his solutions. In that one hour, sixty people completely reinvented their vision of the company. What was also very rewarding was to see how good they felt about being part of the process; to see them fully participate and wake up to the world of endless possibilities. In fact, sometimes groups have to be reined in, as individuals' imaginations can carry them so far from the original objective that they end up transporting their companies into other business realms that traditionally have not been part of their remit. And I have yet to see the practice of this exercise, or variations on it, draw a blank.

If you find it impossible to create a solution to a particular problem, write it down and share it with a colleague or friend. A fresh mind can often see a solution that you would never have imagined. And there *is* almost always a solution. Sometimes it may require only a small change in attitude. When you're dealing with a situation over which you have no control – such as traffic, weather, or interest rates – a change in attitude can help you put it in perspective. Of course, there will always be the rare instance where no contingency plan exists, or where all options have been exhausted, and the only possible outcome is failure. People sometimes say, 'Failure is not an option.' But failure is always an option, unfortunately. What matters is how we respond to it. That is the measure of our character and of our resolve to succeed in the future.

> **The gem cannot be polished without friction, nor the man perfected without trials.**
>
> *Chinese proverb*

Never forget that many of the most successful individuals in history have in common the experience of defeat. They have known failure; they have known rock bottom. And what they've all done – as the song says – is picked themselves up, dusted themselves down and started all over again.


## Be consistent

Your plan is one part of the process of your eventual success. Equally critical is a consistent self-belief, a conviction that you are going to succeed. This means that the plan is not just something you say or write down: it is something you live, twenty-four hours a day.

Act in a manner consistent with success; act as if the success you desire is already a reality; act, speak and think like a winner. Try hard to achieve this consistency; if you do it, it will inform all aspects of your behaviour and, equally importantly, influence others' perception of you.

I had been out of work for a while, many years ago, and was suddenly brought up short against the reality of it – I had no money. I called a friend and told him that I needed a job, and was thinking of approaching a certain company but I didn't know the managing director. 'Oh, he's a lovely fellow,' my friend replied. 'Give him a call and make an appointment – he'll see anyone.' I rang at once. As it was lunchtime I got straight through and we made a date. The day before my appointment I called my friend and asked him how to play the meeting. He told me to dress casually, act lively and speak loudly (because the MD was hard of hearing).

Confidently armed with this information, I turned up next day at his office casually dressed, talking at the top of my voice, and with all the energy of an American games show host on speed. I went into my pitch about who I was and what I had been doing and what I would like to talk to him about, and after a minute and a half of this non-stop onslaught, he put his hand up in a 'Slow down, here' gesture and said, 'Stop! Who are you?' I told him. And then we talked for forty more minutes in a perfectly normal manner, at the end of which he offered me a job and I stayed there for three years.

The twist is that I found out later that my friend had been joking (some friend!), but I just hadn't realised. The MD never saw people he didn't know, didn't like people who were too casual or extrovert, and he most certainly wasn't deaf! Yet I was so convinced that I had inside information that it gave me the self-assurance to act in the manner that is so essential to true success – even if my performance that day was a little over the top. On that occasion, my self-belief was consistent with my goal.

Think of it this way. Imagine walking down the road with your fly buttons open – but you don't know it. You're strolling happily along, talking to your friend, looking into shop windows. And you walk along like this for, let's say, ten minutes. Now imagine somebody pointing out to you that your fly is undone, and then asking you to carry on down the road for another ten minutes. How would you feel? How would you act? Very differently from how you acted when you believed your fly was closed, I think. The point here is that if you truly believe something, how you talk, how you behave and how you think will all be consistent with that belief. So behave as if you believe in your plan. If, on the other hand, your actions are at odds with it, don't expect much progress.

> **I find that the harder I work, the more luck I seem to have.**
>
> *Thomas Jefferson (1743–1826)*

Finally, imagine you have won a wonderful prize, and the award ceremony is going to take place in one month's time. You have been told you are going to get the award, you have read the letter confirming it. You have had your hand shaken and your back slapped – everyone has congratulated you. How are you going to feel and act for the remainder of the month? Will you act reticently or nervously? No! Of course not! You will act in a manner that is consistent with your knowledge.

And so it should be with our own future goals. Believe that they exist in the future, and act accordingly. Your self-belief will manifest itself both in your inner confidence and in your actions.

## Enthusiasm

True enthusiasm is a marvellous quality. It's infectious: it gives confidence to those around you as well as to yourself. When you are putting your plan together, enter into it with gusto. It will be a powerful reinforcement to your commitment. When you speak to others of your goals, speak with that same enthusiasm, that expression of inner exuberance, an unquenchable positive outlook and an assured belief in your future.

Enthusiasm animates, gives life to our plans. Conceiving and designing our plans without it is like building a powerful engine and then having no fuel put in it.

When I first began to speak at conferences, I concentrated so hard on the content of my talk and on the act of memorising it that when I got up to speak I seemed to have forgotten my passion for the subject. I was putting perfect content and presentation before delivery. I corrected this by putting in bold print at the top of every page of my notes: 'Enthusiasm and Passion'. I have now dispensed with that little reminder, but those early experiences taught me that when I communicated with real enthusiasm and passion – to audiences, friends, colleagues – I got my message over much more effectively. I don't mean that you have to be extrovert or loud or brash. But if you show your enthusiasm, your joyful belief, in the absolute achievability of your goal, your success will start to become a reality.

> **When a man dies, if he can pass enthusiasm along to his children, he has left them an estate of incalculable value.**
>
> *Thomas Edison*

Enthusiasm also engages our commitment, because commitment is a personal matter, even at the corporate level. I have spoken to businesses that say, 'We are a committed company!' But I don't fully understand what that means. I know that *individuals* can be committed, but surely a company can be committed only if every individual shares the corporate vision, the corporate plan? Therefore, what I do believe is that companies can be made up of committed individuals. Take this as an example. A company can have the best research and development, the best marketing, the best advertising and the best product; but if the person I speak to when I visit the company has a negative attitude and would rather be somewhere else, then any amount of corporate vision and commitment to excellence will all be for nothing. But if the first person I speak to is enthusiastic, interested and personally committed to presenting his or her company in its best possible light, it can make up for a host of other deficiencies. The bottom line is: people do business with people.

True enthusiasm is free and abundant. It may be that, when you begin to draw up your personal plan, no matter how simple or how ambitious, the only two things that you can generate for yourself are your enthusiasm and your commitment. But when enthusiasm and commitment take root within a project, that project comes to life.

## Opinions versus facts

Once when I was running a course with a colleague, I started to pick out some faults in a proposal of his that I was looking at. 'Robin,' he said, 'opinions are like noses – everybody's got one.' In fact, his actual words were slightly less polite, but the message was quite clear. All too often, when we are discussing our goals with friends or putting a strategy together in a business situation, somebody will make a glib comment based, perhaps, on some personal experience or hidden personal agenda. Unless everyone is vigilant and scrupulous in this respect, it's very easy for an ill-considered comment to transform itself before our eyes into a 'fact', unchecked, unchallenged and possibly quite destructive.

I can recall many meetings where a loose comment has sent the whole mood, the whole discussion, off at a tangent, causing a poor decision to be reached on the basis of one person's opinion. It is extremely important, when you are creating your plan, to work only with facts. The born winner within the child learning to walk works exclusively with facts. Children use tried and tested information to reach their conclusions; they are too young to have been exposed to opinions that can rob them of their goal. This may seem as obvious as the nose on your face, but I am amazed how many plans are nipped in the bud by a glib comment, by 'an opinion'. Of course, considered, informed opinion can be of great value, but it is still no substitute for fact, for accurate information.

All too often we decide not to do something because, at a critical moment, somebody said it wasn't possible – and we chose to believe that person's opinion rather than believe in ourselves.

For example, suppose you decided that you want to start your own business and work for yourself. It's going to involve something you've always been interested in – say, interior design – and you don't know a great deal about it, but your friends say you've got very good taste. They've always been very encouraging about your abilities in this area, and one day you tell them you've decided to set up on your own. Now, I don't know what your friends are like, but I'm pretty sure their reactions will range from 'Fantastic!' to 'You're crazy!' Even your best-intentioned friends may say, 'You've got terrific taste, but you know, you're not really a professional.' Personally, I believe that professionals are always previously unpaid amateurs, who just happened one day to be offered some money for their services. I'm not suggesting, should there be any interior designers reading this book, that theirs is an easy business to get into, but I bet they'll agree that there came a day in their life when they had to make that first decision to go professional; and that what they wanted then is what you would best benefit from when you have to make *your* decision: encouragement. So if your friends' reactions are positive, take them on board; if they're negative, don't take too much notice of them.

Since it's fact that's important, not opinion, seek professional help. Go and find out what you need to do to become an accredited interior designer. Discover what sort of courses you need to go on, what contacts you need to make, who to speak to. Make all this part of your plan. Go and see professional interior designers, write down the questions you want to ask them, ask to see samples from their portfolios. If you don't have a portfolio of your own, ask them how to go about putting one together. Above all, don't let your good idea stall just because somebody said it's impossible.

Facts, not opinions. I remember an occasion when the difference between the two was really brought home to me. It was when I was a student back in the late 70s, and I was at a rugby club summer barbecue, wearing my best flares. I was returning from the bar at some point when I spilt some beer down a friend's jacket – not a whole pint, but quite enough – and I said to him flippantly, 'Ah, well – that colour doesn't suit you anyway.' (It was lime green, if I remember.) 'I'm going to give you a beer shampoo!' he said as he turned to face me, then proceeded to pour the contents of his glass over my head. When I said that his jacket didn't suit him, I was simply expressing an opinion. When he said he was going to pour the beer over my head, he was expressing a fact.

## Do it now

In the last chapter I asked you to choose three things which, if success were guaranteed, you would wish for. I'm sure you had no difficulty in choosing them. The next step, now, is to actually draw up your plan. Sit down, take those three wishes, work out for each of them exactly what it is you want to achieve, then ask yourself when you want it to happen. Put together a time-scale: short-term, medium- or long-term – you decide. Now, what do you have to do to make it happen? What skills do you need to learn? What problems or obstacles are you likely to encounter along the way? What benefits will the achievement of this goal bring to your life? How will you feel when you have achieved it? These are questions you have to identify and ask. Answering them will bring your plan fully alive for you.

You'll think that I've said this often enough already, perhaps, but the fact is that it would be impossible to overemphasise the importance of writing your plan down. A written plan is such a powerfully remembered tool. Lodged in your subconscious mind, it will stay with you twenty-four hours a day, seven days a week, until your goal is achieved. Remember, it was those Yale students who wrote their life goals down who succeeded in their chosen careers, while the others owed more to chance than to design. I hardly need to tell you by now that this book is all about designing success, about creating your own blueprint, and that the creation of your plan is critical to the success of your goal. So when is the right time to put this plan into practice? Now! (You *knew* I'd say that.) Right now! Not tomorrow – today!

When you get to the end of this chapter, I shall ask you to sit down and write out your goals. This is what I shall ask you to do then: write down your reasons for *not* attempting them; write down your reasons *for* attempting them; next, concentrate only on the positive reasons and on the benefits of achieving your goals; then, set your targets for each stage along the way.

You will be able to change the dates if you need to, you'll be able to change the plan – that's fine – but what is crucial is that you put it into action now! Any delay now will stall your momentum, undermine your ambition, dilute your enthusiasm and commitment. How many times have you heard people say, 'I'm going to start my own business soon but right now I'm figuring out all the angles, I'm looking into things, I'm checking it out'? All they are doing is stalling – stopping themselves from getting started – because as long as they don't start they can't fail; they are still in their comfort zone.

So take that plan and start your journey now.

**My own experience has taught me this: if you wait for the perfect moment when all is safe and assured it may never arrive. Mountains will not be**

**climbed, races won or lasting happiness achieved.**
*Maurice Chevalier (1888–1972), French singer and*
*film actor*

Before moving on to the next chapter, do the following exercise. Identify three goals – one short-term, one medium-term and one long-term. Take your notebook and write them down. Your short-term goal can be something you hope to achieve in one month or less. Your medium-term one can take up to a year to achieve, and your long-term goal can take any amount of time as long as it's more than a year – you decide how long long-term is for you. Underneath your three goals draw two columns. Then write down in column 1 all the reasons why you should not attempt these goals, all the reasons you *shouldn't* try; and in column 2 list all the reasons why you *should* try. Now take a red pen, look at both of the columns, and cross out all the negative reasons.

This will leave you with only the positive reasons. Next, determine what you will have to achieve at each stage so that you will be able to measure your successful progress towards your goal. Say your short-term target is simply to be more encouraging to those with whom you work – which might seem a strange ambition, but it would be a big step if it involved changing a pattern of behaviour that you don't much like. Your goal for the first week might be that every day you'll praise one person, you'll find a reason to say, 'Well done' or 'That was good', and observe his response. In week 2, you'll determine to take the time to see one colleague from your department and say to her: 'I really appreciate all the work you've done in the last couple of years but I've never had the chance to tell you – so I just wanted to tell you now.' In the third week, you'll continue to do what you've done in the first and second, but you'll go that bit further by inviting somebody to lunch, just to say, 'Well done' and to give yourself a chance to know him better. And by the end of the fourth week, whatever your short-term goal may be, you'll look back over the last month and feel a tremendous sense of achievement when you realise how far you have come.

How often have you done something new in your life, like learning to ski, to swim, to drive or to speak a foreign language, and thought, 'That wasn't so difficult – I wish I'd done it sooner!' Well, don't wait until later because now is sooner. Do it now!

# 7 Confidence

Confidence – or lack of it – is something we can all recognise in others, and if we are honest with ourselves we know whether we are truly confident or not. It is an intangible quality, not something you can take a pill for, but it's one that you can and should develop. A personal commitment to developing your confidence is a major investment in your future.

Your self-confidence is a direct indicator of how you feel about yourself. The relationship that you have with yourself is the single most important relationship you will ever have. It is the basis on which you are able to form other relationships. To say that somebody lacks confidence suggests a flaw in their personality, a natural deficiency which inhibits their success; yet in fact our confidence is something we have power over. We can develop it, build it up, and use it to help us create our future.

Confidence is to do with the ability to believe in something without necessarily having any firm evidence for it. The ability to believe in yourself is the foundation of your confidence, and positive experiences serve to reinforce it. I remember when the English football team had to play against Scotland in the 1996 Euro Cup, and after a long absence, the Scots were coming down to Wembley Stadium to play the 'auld enemy'. They were desperate to win and the English were desperate not to lose. Terry Venables and his English team had been treated so negatively by the media that you felt their confidence had to be at an all-time low.

Once the game began the Scots played as always, with

a great deal of passion; and the English defended well. Then the Scots were awarded a penalty, which they missed. Later in the first half, at the other end of the stadium, Paul Gascoigne chipped the ball over the head of a Scottish defender and on the volley kicked it into the back of the net. It was one of the best goals I ever have seen.

What happened then was extraordinary: there was an immediate surge in the team's energy, as though a light had been switched on, with every English player showing a renewed belief in their collective ability. You could almost see the transformation: it was as if they grew an extra inch. Their self-belief, their confidence in what they were capable of, had been fully awakened; and as history went on to show, they won the game. In the next round they absolutely thrashed Holland, then they beat Spain on penalties. Then, in the semi-finals of the competition they met the one team in the world which, though it has less imagination, has more self-confidence than any other – Germany.

What does Germany do when it goes a goal down in a match? They all huddle down, look at the situation, and determine to score two more goals; and that's normally what the situation requires. In this match they equalised. Did any English fan, when the game came dramatically to a penalty shoot-out, imagine that a German player was going to stub his foot on the ground? Have his shorts fall down in the run-up? Or balloon the kick over the top post? No – such eventualities are almost unimaginable, because from their years of experience the Germans have developed a supreme inner confidence that they manifest externally. Every player in the German team believed that day that they were going to win. I think that, by contrast, for many years both the English and Scottish teams had merely *hoped* that they would.

Self-confidence makes all the difference. I once met a man who had spent seven years in the 1960s as a deep-sea diver in the Royal Navy. I asked him if he had ever been afraid of something going wrong when he was alone two hundred feet under water with just an old bell-helmet on and an air pipe to link him with the surface. 'No,' he replied. 'I'd done emergency training.' He spoke these words with such a conviction that made it quite obvious that his training had entirely removed any fears he might have had and given him an absolute confidence about his safety.

**A belief is not merely an idea that the mind possesses, it is an idea that possesses the mind.**
*Robert Bolton*

We need to create within ourselves the confidence to deal with any mishap that may come along while we are pursuing our dreams of success.

Have you ever noticed a child making a speech? Children are often astonishingly confident; they can stand up in front of a room full of strangers because they haven't yet learned to be afraid. Other people's opinions don't concern them. They've got a good enough opinion of themselves, almost never having negative self-beliefs. New companies, when they start up, frequently exhibit this confident mentality in the market-place; they are young, ambitious, and energetic. However, the dividing line between an enabling confidence and a fatal arrogance is at times very fine, and we need to recognise the difference.

In this chapter we shall look at ways of developing self-confidence. I believe that the key to this lies in the setting and achieving of simple goals. When you do this, you develop in yourself a belief that you can achieve; it helps you to build up your self-image; and it gives you the feeling, and allows you to understand, that you are able to take control.

They say that nothing succeeds like success; and the confidence that success brings is indeed self-perpetuating. I believe you have the ability to develop your confidence to the levels that success demands – and, who knows, maybe win a world championship along the way.

## You can if you think you can

I keep returning to Henry Ford's 'If you think you can or you think you can't, you're usually right.' I love this sentiment because for me it's so true. When I look back at my life so far, the things I have achieved are the things I believed I could achieve, and the things I believed would never happen, never have. Why is this? It's because, as I said before, when we create an image in our minds of a future outcome, our subconscious then naturally works towards it; with no conscious awareness on our part, it quietly seeks to fulfil our vision.

So when you believe you can, you have created a positive image, one of success; and when you believe you can't, you have created a negative image, one of defeat.

> **According to the theory of aerodynamics, the bumble-bee is unable to fly. This is because the size, weight and shape of its body in relation to the total wing spread make flying impossible. But the bumble-bee, being ignorant of these profound scientific truths, goes ahead and flies anyway and also manages to make a little honey every day.**
>
> *Anon.*

For evidence, look at the self-belief, the self-confidence, of success-oriented people. One thing they think – no, truly believe – is that they can achieve extraordinary goals. When Roger Bannister ran the four-minute mile in 1954 he was the first person ever to break what was previously believed to be an impossible barrier; and yet since he made that breakthrough over twenty-seven thousand people have followed in his wake. He didn't just break a record: he broke a limiting belief that many had held to be a fact. Mount Everest, first conquered in 1953 after countless failed attempts, has since been climbed so often that you can now take organised guided tours that, if you are willing to pay the price, and all things being well, will get you to the top.

But don't feel you have to go and climb Mount Everest: we all have our own Everest to climb, and you know what yours is. Identify it and get ready to climb it.

When I was about nine we lived in a big rambling house with a three-car garage that was always full of unwanted junk that we had accumulated over the years. One day when it was raining and I had nothing to do, my mother suggested I go and tidy it up. I went in and took a look at it: it was so full of stuff that there was barely space for one car. I set about tidying and sweeping, and even began to build a bonfire nearby. After four or five hours I still hadn't made much of an impact, and I was tired. When my father arrived and asked me how I was getting on, I said, 'Not bad', and I particularly remember my mother saying, 'Robin will finish this because whenever he says he'll do something, he always does.'

Now this may have been a clever piece of psychology on my mother's part, but in any event it had a great impact on me. Throughout my life it's been the case, whatever I've started I've finished, be it a journey, a marathon or a garage to be cleaned out. I have always had a firm confidence in my ability to endure, and when I commit to things I see them through to completion.

The things in my life that I have failed to achieve have been those things that I've believed I would fail at; there have been no surprises.

> **Come to the edge, He said. They said: we are afraid. Come to the edge, He said. They came. He pushed them and they flew.**
> *Guillaume Apollinaire (1880–1918), French poet*

When we face new challenges or set new goals, we need to believe absolutely that we can meet them, accomplish them. But in all our endeavours, even with the firmest self-belief it's natural for doubts to surface; it's natural to have moments of worry and fear. I remember a famous television star who used to get terrified before every show. He suffered from the kind of anxiety that is quite natural among performers, but his was particularly acute, and every night the show's producer would have to listen to an endless refrain of 'Tonight I *know* it's going to go wrong', 'This is the night they'll discover I have absolutely no talent', and so on. But as soon as the clock neared count-down, the performer would rise to the occasion as always and go on and wow the audience.

Self-doubt is natural, even for someone who's had twenty years of success at the top of his profession; but the important thing is to put that self-doubt into perspective. Understand that everyone has these moments, and don't fear them or let them immobilise you.

**Self-doubt is nature's way of giving us a reality check.**

See beyond your self-doubt and understand, as you persevere in the pursuit of your goals, that it's a natural experience in the change process that is part of your journey to success. Is there anyone who hasn't thought, 'What if I make a fool of myself?', 'What if I fail?' Don't let negative thinking undermine your resolve; positive self-belief and a determination to succeed will always overcome it.

When you set out on a personal quest, it's natural enough to ask yourself, 'How can I be sure I'll succeed?' The answer is, you can never be one hundred per cent certain that you'll succeed. You might just as well ask yourself, 'How can I be sure I'll fail?' The truth is that there are no certainties in life. Failure and success are both thoughts that exist in your mind, and it's the one you choose to believe in that will become your dominant and determining thought.

**A man who does not think for himself, does not think at all.**

*Oscar Wilde (1854–1900)*

So many of us, when we face the future, are dominated by memories of our past failures: 'Oh, I'll never manage that', or 'No point in applying for *that* job – I'll never get it.' But don't allow self-doubt to get a grip on you in this way, or fear to overtake you. Think confidently and believe that you *can* achieve, and then you will automatically behave according to that belief.

## Have faith in yourself

Faith has been described as a belief that runs ahead of the evidence. Anyone who has been exposed to formal religion, or even informal religion, will be well aware of the emphasis that is placed on faith, on belief in things unseen. The confidence you need to achieve the future you want depends on your faith in yourself. If you create a positive self-belief, with faith, you are maximising your potential to create success.

Those negative beliefs that are holding you back were formed from your past experiences. They are the result of learned behaviour, and you can *un*learn them. But it's no good thinking you can change them at the drop of a hat, that you can randomly construct another set of behaviours without solid foundation. It is crucial to your lasting success, to your happiness and satisfaction, that your belief in your abilities should be consistent with your fundamental core values, and your core values are personal ethical and moral standards by which you measure yourself. Work against them, and you work against yourself.

The Oracle at Delphi is a shrine seventy miles north-west of Athens where, at the time of Socrates, people went on pilgrimage in order to ask important questions and receive answers of the gods. Above the Oracle is written 'Know thyself.' Without getting too philosophical, it's worth asking yourself these questions: 'Who am I?' 'What do I want out of life?' 'What do I believe?' and 'What do I believe I can achieve?'

As you create that faith in yourself, so your confidence develops. Companies use 'mission statements' to help create faith in themselves. Almost every major organisation I have worked with has printed in its annual report a mission statement clearly defining its values. It shows that the company knows what it believes in, what it is seeking to achieve and how it is going to achieve it. It doesn't matter whether it's a small family outfit or a major telecommunications company – the mission statement clearly defines the value system of the business.

So what is your personal mission statement, what are your values? The route to success is not a long, straight road with clear signposts at every junction. It can be a smooth three-lane motorway one moment, then a twisting, fog-enveloped mountain path the next. Suddenly lost, you feel at your most vulnerable and uncertain at such times. But it is at these very times that your determination and imagination, your unfailing faith in yourself, carry you through. Belief in yourself and in your values will always give you direction and enable you to find a way, even through the darkest moments.

## Remember the child

We are born without prejudice and without any sense of externally imposed limits on our potential. We are born genetically conditioned to succeed in the face of natural adversity, to survive. We enter this world as natural-born winners.

**We can easily forgive a child who is afraid of the dark; the real tragedy of life is when adults are afraid of the light.**

*Plato (c. 427–347 BC), Greek philosopher*

Children are born with such imagination, such inner confidence, that in their minds they are the heroes of a thousand adventures. When that imagination and confidence are encouraged, anything seems possible; but when they are neglected, the child is damaged for life. We have seen the tragic television pictures of the Romanian orphanages and scenes of Third World deprivation, where children are left uncared for, without stimulation, without love. If a child's imagination is not developed, if the confidence she should naturally acquire is not fed, she will have no memory of personal accomplishment and hence no personal confidence. Happily, most of us did experience that sense of accomplishment as children, and the memories of it remain with us, however deeply buried. As we grow older, we seem to forget and afford no real value to those qualities which as children gave us that absolute conviction in our ability to succeed.

So put yourself in touch with the child you were: feel again the sense of wonderment and the belief that anything is possible.

When a child sets herself a goal she may have no prior knowledge or experience of success; she just believes she can do it – whatever it is. The resources she draws on are her imagination and determination. You have still got that imagination; and though sometimes you may need to dig deep to find the determination, you've still got that too. And just as a child's confidence grows through praise and positive experiences, so does yours. So make it an ongoing process – feel good about yourself and about your personal achievements; and if you do something well, something that pleases you, give yourself a quiet, 'Well done!'

# Put setbacks into perspective

I find it odd when I see somebody with a flat tyre or who has just spilt a glass of milk getting upset and losing their temper. Life and death are life and death, and we should treat them as such; everything else should be put into perspective. It reminds me of the story of the American tourist on holiday in the north of Scotland, who asked an old fellow sitting on a wall, 'What's the weather going to be like tomorrow?' Without looking at the sky, the old man replied, 'The kind of weather I like.' The tourist tried again, 'Is it going to be sunny?' 'I don't know,' was the reply. 'Well, is it going to rain?' 'Wouldn't know about that.' By now the visitor was pretty perplexed. 'OK,' he said, 'if it's the kind of weather you like, what kind of weather is it going to be?' The old man looked at the American and answered, 'I learned long ago that I had no control over the weather, so I taught myself to like whatever weather comes along.'

Moral: don't get upset about things you have no control over. You have the power to determine your emotional response to events. If you *don't* control them, they have a habit of controlling you.

So don't act as if the spilt milk is a life-and-death matter, or get seriously stressed out by a flat tyre; they've happened, they're a setback. But they are small setbacks, and everybody gets them. It's what you do next that's important. Whatever you are seeking to achieve at this moment, whether it's building up a company or preparing a simple dinner-party for close friends, things can, and probably will, go wrong. If the toast falls the wrong way, if you miss out on a promotion, put it into perspective. Otherwise, it will diminish your commitment to succeed. It's not what happens to you that matters; it's what you do about it.

When a setback occurs, don't identify with it. Use it simply as something to learn from.

**Fail fast and fail often.**
*Thomas Watson (1874–1956), founder of IBM*

At seventeen years old Boris Becker stunned the world in 1985 by winning at Wimbledon as an unseeded player. He came back a year later and successfully defended his title. The year after that at the age of nineteen on an outside court he lost to an unknown in the second round, and was out. At the press conference afterwards he was asked how he felt. With a wisdom way in advance of his years, Becker replied, 'Look, nobody died – I just lost a tennis match.'

He got it in perspective: it was just a tennis match. Sure, it was Wimbledon; sure, the prize was wonderful; but it wasn't a matter of life or death.

Once when I was very worried about something and a friend asked me, 'Robin, what were you worrying about a year ago today?' I looked at him, baffled, and said, 'I've no idea – why?' 'Well,' he said, 'a year from today you won't remember this either.' Try asking yourself the same question: think, what exactly *were* you worrying about a year ago today? Can you actually remember? I think probably not.

When something bad happens to you – when a love affair goes wrong or a business plan blows up or the bank suddenly decides to call in a loan – you can, if you choose to, hold on to the experience. You can identify with it, decide to carry it around with you for the rest of your life, like a piece of unwanted baggage. But if you do keep those negative memories and their associated feelings and allow them to influence your self-image, all you will do is handicap yourself. The alternative is in your control: simply learn from the experience, then leave it behind. In other words, drop the baggage.

**No one can make you feel inferior without your consent.**
*Eleanor Roosevelt (1884–1962)*

The grandmother of a certain friend of mine was, I'm sorry to say, a most lamentable woman. In all the years I knew her, she never smiled; she delighted in other people's misfortune; she was, in fact, a very bitter woman. It turned out that once as a young girl she had been getting ready to go to a dance when her father told her to stay at home and look after her younger brother. On that day, she later told my friend's mother, she determined never to enjoy herself again. It was her way of punishing her father, of showing him how miserable he had made her. All those years later, the memories of that evening had become her reality: they had become the bag she had carried around with her for the rest of her life. All she had was her bitterness. I'm trying to show you how very important it is to leave this kind of baggage behind, because if you don't move on, if you don't learn from the lessons that life offers you, life has a knack of delivering other, more painful, lessons, until finally you get the message – or not, even never at all, as in the case of my friend's grandmother.

Pay attention to your negative patterns of behaviour – we all have them – negative habits that help to generate failure. So try and identify them, and think about how to change them.

Finally, prepare for setbacks, so that when they occur you are at least emotionally prepared. And when you do hit one, look for the positive. Of course, there are some tragedies from which it is impossible to glean anything positive at all; but one thing my cancer really made me aware of was how much I loved my family – and I had never taken the time to tell them so. It also determined me to stop wasting time and start living my dreams. When I left hospital I set about fulfilling many of them, and am continuing to do so.

So think of a personal setback that in the end had a happy outcome, and draw strength from it when another setback occurs. Remind yourself that when bad things happen, in the end it's not always for the worst.

## Become your own coach

Do you remember being encouraged by a teacher, a friend or a colleague in something that was important to you? Think back to that moment: how did it feel? I bet it felt pretty good, because at that moment somebody expressly believed in you. They believed you could achieve, and they let you know they did by positively affirming their belief. In the process they helped you build your confidence, your self-image – just as a coach does in sport. Of course, coaches also help examine strategies and focus on finer points of technique, but I believe the great coaches finally motivate by encouragement.

Émile Coué, the French pharmacist and psycho-therapist referred to in chapter 3, was one day asked for a prescription medicine by a very insistent patient who didn't actually have a prescription. Knowing he couldn't dispense the medicine anyway, Coué gave him a sugar pill instead, telling him it was an even better remedy than the one he'd asked for. Some days later the man returned, full of gratitude, saying he had made a full recovery and felt wonderful. Realising that it could only be the patient's own belief in getting well that had cured him, Coué set about creating a method of helping people to benefit from the power of positive self-suggestion – and enabled himself, in the process, to do away with sugar pills. In due course, he devised his now well known formula for those recovering from illness: they should say aloud twenty times a day, 'Every day in every way I'm getting better and better.'

As we know, what the mind believes to be true is held deep in the subconscious. The repetition of 'Every day in every way I am getting better and better' enhanced Coué's patients' recovery. And it worked not only for those who were suffering from psychosomatic problems, but also for others who had clinical illnesses.

Coaches are very good at putting positive affirmations into the minds of the people they work with. So why not become your own coach? Think of it, think of yourself being your own encourager. Think of what a coach would say, if you had one, when you have challenges to face, obstacles to overcome, even just simple tasks to achieve. What would your coach say? Well, you haven't got a coach, so make it your job to say these things yourself. I remember, when I was training for a marathon, entering a three-mile race as a build-up. Now, I'll make no bones about it: I'm flat-footed and I couldn't honestly compare my technique with that of a top-grade Kenyan marathon runner. Anyway, before the end of the second mile I had been lapped. It was a one-mile circuit, with guides posted at intervals to make sure the runners stayed on course. Towards the end of the race, when most of the entrants had already passed the finishing line and I was still running with just one or two others behind me, as I passed each guide there would be a small burst of applause or a few shouts of encouragement. And I remember what a real difference it made. It put a fresh spring in my step and made me determine not to stop running until I got there.

Be encouraged by your successes. Carry the memories of them close to your heart, and when a new challenge presents itself, recall them. And as well as becoming your own encourager, your own coach, why not do the same for friends or colleagues? You can do it as subtly as seems appropriate. A senior partner of a large organisation once told me that she ruled her department with an iron hand – and it was, to all intents and purposes, a successful department. But she acknowledged that along the way she might have lost some of her humanity. She was so driven by results that all that mattered was performance. When I asked her why she didn't encourage her staff, she simply said that she had never been encouraged herself, had had to do it the tough way, and that it had worked for her. So together we sat down and set a simple goal: each day she would take the time to appreciate the efforts of two people. This wouldn't call for gushing praise or anything else that might sound insincere; just a quiet word of acknowledgement would be sufficient. 'Don't pay so much attention to how the other person responds, but to how you feel,' I told her. A month later when I asked her how she felt, she said, 'Great!' Everyone had noticed a difference, the mood of the whole department had lifted, and people were working more confidently. So she felt good about that – and about herself.

The process of coaching within an organisation becomes a self-generating process. It is not all about delivering one-off battle-winning pep talks and psyching people up; it's about acknowledging them, about quietly and consistently appreciating their efforts, and helping them strive towards greater successes.

## Developing your resources

I said earlier that it is worth thinking about who your heroes are and identifying which of their qualities you most admire. Having identified them, you can then consciously seek to develop those qualities within your own pattern of behaviour. Cary Grant was once asked how it was that he was always so charming. He replied that, whenever he met somebody with a quality he found endearing, whether it was courtesy, humility, a natural kindness or anything else, he simply adopted it for him-self. He emulated the qualities he most admired in others.

Be on the lookout for people who have achieved what it is you want to achieve, and ask their advice. See the help they can give you as another resource, and aim to develop all your assets in the pursuit of your personal success.

Do you read much? Statistics suggest that less than 10 per cent of the population read more than two books a year. Now, if you were to read four books a year you would have read twice as many as 90 per cent of the population! If you go to any bookstore you will find a personal-development or self-help section. Taking the time to read a book that will help you to gain an insight into something you are seeking to do cannot be time badly spent. If you wanted to learn to cook Thai food, you would think nothing of buying a book on Thai cookery; if you wanted to redesign your garden you would probably buy a book or a videotape that would give you the instruction and knowledge you needed.

So it should be with self-help. Build up a library of books on the subject. Listen to tapes in the car or when you are out walking. Books and tapes will give you the knowledge and the basis from which to create, but only the application of that knowledge will give you the experience you need and produce the results. Talk to people who have done the sort of thing that you are seeking to do, and learn from *their* experience. So continue to ask yourself these two important questions: 'Who do I need to talk to?' and 'What do I need to find out?' In this way you will always develop the resources you need to achieve your goals.

## Overcome your anxiety

We have all felt fear in our lives from time to time, but for many people it's a constant low-level condition, a state of near-permanent non-specific anxiety. Fear in itself is a natural response; it saved our forefathers from being eaten by grizzly bears and sabre-toothed tigers. However, prolonged sensations of fear lead to long-term anxiety, which is a very debilitating condition. It strips you of your self-confidence and your self-esteem, and makes you fearful of the future. You can be almost paralysed by worry about the future, because you have no concept of what it holds. None of us do. But what you tend to forget is that all these feelings of fear exist solely in your head. Think of it this way. *You* put them there, *you* nurtured them and now you are giving them free range of your mind. But you *can* overcome these fears, and you can take steps to do it right now.

**He who fears he will suffer, already suffers from his fear.**
*Michel de Montaigne (1533–92), French essayist*

Anxiety is not a modern phenomenon. The full version of the Lord's Prayer includes the line, 'Protect us from all anxiety.' But if you don't deal with your anxiety and control it, it will ultimately control you, leading to a sense of worthlessness and self-pity, and even possibly to depression.

For many years I suffered from panic attacks but didn't understand why. At the age of twenty-eight I decided that they were going to ruin my life or I was going to have to do something about them. After much searching I found a book called *Self Help for Your Nerves* by Dr Claire Weekes. The understanding that book gave me – the insight into what I was experiencing, the realisation that there was a very logical explanation for it – had a remarkable effect. It immediately disarmed the emotion that had been so painfully holding me back. I mention this here because I know from personal experience that many people do feel a non-specific anxiety for which they can't articulate the cause. What has actually happened is that they have become anxious about becoming anxious, or are anxious about the possibility of having a panic attack. This condition is known as precipitatory anxiety: because your experience of that condition is that it always comes back, even when you are not actually feeling panicky you are anxious about it until you just *know* it's going to. And sure enough, in one of life's cruellest self-fulfilling prophecies, it does.

**Anxiety is a thin stream of fear trickling through the mind. If encouraged, it cuts a channel into which all other thoughts are drained.**
*Arthur Somers Roche*

Leave these negative thoughts behind. Think how much energy you are using up in these feelings of fear and anxiety. Imagine if that energy were being used instead to create positive, life-enhancing affirmations of success.

It is natural and healthy to worry, to have moments of self-doubt. A degree of nervous anticipation heightens awareness when going for a new job, say, or going on a first date. But if you are convinced in advance that something bad will occur – that you won't get the job, that the date will be a disaster – your nervousness will run away with you and it's odds on that you'll be right. Fear can become a paralysing force in our lives if it strips us of our confidence, of our self-belief. It can develop into a debilitating mental condition.

I remember when I had Hodgkin's disease, driving myself down to the Royal Marsden Hospital and checking myself into the ward. I was given a bed by the window in this small four-bed room. The night before the operation, a friend and his father unexpectedly turned up to say hello, then a member of my family dropped in. But by eight o'clock I was on my own. The lights went down and I tried to sleep, but I was somewhat preoccupied. Around midnight ambulancemen brought a man in on a stretcher and put him in the bed beside mine. He was breathing through an oxygen mask, and complained of being intolerably hot, though it was the middle of December. I offered to swap beds so he could be by the window, telling the nurse that I had no objection to it being opened if that would make him more comfortable. It was not possible, the nurse said, but he thanked me anyway.

It was then that I saw him properly. He was about thirty-five, there were tumours on his face, and he was obviously gravely ill. Next day he told me that he had had cancer for two years, but no treatments had been able to stop it spreading. He had tumours throughout his body and, having had a total blood transfusion, he was now in for a body blast of radiotherapy – a last-ditch attempt, he said.

In due course I was taken in for my operation, then stayed in the high dependency unit for two and a half days. When I came back to the ward his bed was occupied by someone else.

As soon as I was able to get up I started exploring. I was shuffling along the corridor with numerous tubes in different parts of my body, looking a bit like Frankenstein's monster, when I happened to look into a single bedroom and saw this fellow now sitting in an armchair. He looked great, and I popped my head in and told him so. He smiled back and said in the most matter-of-fact manner that the doctors had said there was no more they could do for him. And before I could say anything, he added casually that he was off to the hospice the next day.

In the room were his wife, his children and others who I imagined to be close friends and relatives. Some of them were obviously very distressed. Not knowing what to say, I unbuttoned my pyjama top and showed him my scar: 'Look what they did to me,' I said. He grimaced a little: 'That looks terrible.' Then there was a rather embarrassed silence on my part because I knew my condition bore no comparison to his plight. Then he looked at me evenly, and said, 'I want you to get well. I want you to beat cancer because it has beaten me. I want you to even the score or go one up. All the best.' With that I said, 'Don't worry – I will', and I left the room, saddened and upset. I went back to my bed and lay there for a while.

It was only later that I realised that I would never again be as fearful about my health and my future as I had been before that day. Of course, I was anxious about certain treatments and their long-term outcome, but what raised my spirits time and time again was that, whenever I was down or those around me were suffering, we were such a great support to each other. Though he knew that his life was soon to be over and he would be leaving his family behind, that man thought of me, encouraged me to get well.

Most of our anxiety and fear is about things that might happen in the future, things that don't yet exist. Now, should you owe the Mafia money or be on the run from the police, I grant that any fears you may have are well founded; there is a reason for them, and you'll know what that reason is. But most of us aren't in this kind of plight. I cannot recommend strongly enough, if you suffer from any form of anxiety, that you determine to help yourself. Read books, seek guidance, share your problem with friends. This will begin the process of understanding and overcoming it; of putting it behind you, once and for all.

## Abolish negative thoughts

Whatever task we may be facing, it's common to get negative thoughts about the challenge in hand. Maybe it's something as simple as being about to play a game of tennis and thinking, 'Yeah, it will probably rain' or 'I'm bound to lose.' Do not give value to those negative thoughts: they do not define you, they are not a part of you; they are simply thoughts that you allow to exist in your mind. If you do give value to them, they will begin to dominate your outlook. So if you are going to create a dominant thought, make it a positive one.

An advert for one of the military services in America used to have as its slogan 'Be all that you can be.' I like that idea very much: you owe it to yourself to be all that you can be, to realise your fullest potential. And you can start the process now by abolishing your negative thoughts, by simply not dwelling on them. When you have a negative thought, focus immediately on a positive one. They say that if you want others to love you it is important to love yourself. It's equally true that if you want others to believe in you, you must first believe in yourself.

But you will not begin to believe in yourself, or develop

your confidence, by associating with the negative, by thinking yourself to be less worthy or less capable than you truly are. To that end, avoid negative people – people who, whenever you tell them you are going to do something, immediately pour scorn on it or pull a long face. Avoid them. Visualise strongly the success you desire, and when negative thoughts arise simply ignore them. Remember: the you you see is the you you'll be. How you see yourself, how you visualise yourself, is also what you will be seen as, and ultimately become. Fall hostage to negative thoughts and a poor self-image, and you will become a failure. Abolish those thoughts, build strong self-belief and focus on the positive, and you take a huge step towards success.

In the 1991 Rugby World Cup, when Australia were playing Ireland in Dublin in the quarter-final, with minutes to go Ireland scored and went into the lead. The fans in the Lansdowne Road stadium were ecstatic. Australia had entered as the favourites and here they were being beaten by a small nation on their home ground. What happened next was that, as the Irish prepared to take the conversion kick their captain Michael Lynagh took the team behind the goalposts and said to them, 'OK, no panicking, here is what we are going to do. After the kick-off we win the first line-out, then pass the ball through the line to David Campese, who'll score in the corner.' After the kick-off, the line-out duly happened but Campese, realising that he was going to be unable to make the line, flicked the ball to Michael Lynagh and it was he who scored.

The point is that the Australian team did not use that time behind the posts to dwell on the negative, to allow their minds to be overtaken by thoughts of losing in the quarter-finals of the World Cup, that World Cup they had dreamt of winning. They focused clearly on what they were going to do and they did it. They might well not have done it, but because they believed they could and because they visualised clearly the outcome they wanted to achieve, they greatly increased their chances of creating that result. You can do the same thing, and in the process build up the confidence you need to see you through all those future challenges.

# 8   No Fear of Failure

The fourth common feature of success is the absence of all fear of failure. This is not to suggest that we should act like Disney characters, bumbling along with a permanent smile on our faces and regardless of the problems and obstacles that are bound to come our way. But it is important to recognise the difference between those that are real and can harm us, and those that we imagine, those that exist solely in our minds.

When we set out to achieve any goal we begin by visualising a positive outcome. But as we move towards our objective and encounter difficulties en route, it's easy to grow fearful that our desired outcome will not materialise and that as a result we will suffer some harm, be it financial or personal. Often in our lives we are in such a rush to get to where we want to go that we lose sight of exactly where that is, and it's then that we start using loose, vague terms to describe what it is we are trying to achieve. We talk of acquiring security, financial freedom or happiness, or of developing the business. But unless we keep hold of that original clear vision of exactly what it is we want to do, we can easily get lost in the day-to-day problems. They become even larger in our minds, turning ultimately into barriers to our success. As Franklin D. Roosevelt said in 1937, 'We have nothing to fear but fear itself.'

**The truth that many people never understand until it is too late, is that the more you try to avoid suffering the more you suffer, because smaller and more insignificant things begin to torture you in**

**proportion to your fear of being hurt.**
*Thomas Merton (1915–68), American poet and monk*

Many CEOs and self-made millionaires are, by nature, problem-solvers. They look for solutions, not more problems. Their leadership style is based upon sharing the vision of what they are trying to achieve and on looking to the people within their organisation, as well as to themselves, to find the solutions. If you truly believe that you are ultimately going to succeed and are committed to the process, then you too can choose not to identify with problems along the way, but to take the view that come what may you will overcome it. I call this the 'So what?' attitude to failure.

There is a difference between the 'So what?' attitude and the 'Who cares?' attitude. One, determined to succeed, shrugs off failure and gets on with the job in hand. The other is fundamentally alien to success, and in consequence accepts inertia.

It's so important that you care, and it's also important that you have faith in your ability to recover from setbacks. Failure is never final unless you determine it to be so. Walt Disney was bankrupt and recovering from a nervous breakdown when he made *Steamboat Willie Goes to Hollywood*, the cartoon featuring for the first time the character now known as Mickey Mouse. Disney later said that his bankruptcy had afforded him his greatest lesson in life. Financially speaking, when you can recover from that there is nothing else that can keep you down.

When you understand that often the single biggest barrier you face is self-imposed, exists only in your mind, you will find a fresh perspective that sees opportunities more clearly. I don't propose that you neglect your responsibilities or ignore real threats; but I do ask you to differentiate clearly between the real and the imagined.

Be aware of the real; ignore the imagined.

I believe that, when we look at the four features common to success – a clear goal, a definite plan, confidence and no fear of failure – it is the absence of any fear of failure, alongside a clear goal, that stands out as the most important of the four. Fear has the ability to paralyse us into inaction, and all the planning in the world will be unable to overcome that. Our confidence will be stripped, and our goal will be unrealised.

> **It is not the critic who counts; nor the man who points out how the strong stumbled, or where the doer of the deed could have done better. The credit belongs to the man who is actually in the arena; whose face is marred by dust and sweat and blood; who strives valiantly; who errs and comes up short again and again. Who knows the great enthusiasms, the great devotions, and spends himself in a worthy cause; who at the best knows in the end the triumphs of high achievement; and who at the worst, if he fails, at least he fails while daring greatly; so that his place shall never be with those cold and timid souls who know neither victory nor defeat.**
> *Theodore Roosevelt (1858–1919), twenty-sixth American president*

## Don't quit

We have seen how the 'Don't quit' attitude of the winner contributes significantly to his success. Sometimes, when we begin the long journey towards personal success, our determination is our only resource; it may be what keeps us going, our only hope. Look back at your life so far and identify something you very much wanted to achieve, and that through your own efforts and without any assistance you did achieve. That's clearly something to be proud of. All too often, though, when we look to the future we recall only our failures. So look back and clearly identify all the successes you can think of, however small.

And use those memories to boost your belief in your potential to succeed again.

> **Those who try to do something and fail are infinitely better than those who try to do nothing and succeed.**
>
> *Richard Bird*

It is all too easy to quit. It puts off the problems and the suffering until another time; the excuses we come up with seem fully justifiable; and our colleagues and friends are ready to sympathise: 'Don't worry – you'll do better next time.' But in truth you, and perhaps they too, know that 'next time' is a long way off, if ever at all.

But don't give up, don't stop trying to cope with your problems. It's amazing, when you determine to overcome a lifelong fear, how simple action and commitment strengthen your resolve and develop your confidence. And in the process your perceived fear fades into insignificance.

In the 1980 Olympics Sebastian Coe was the clear favourite for the eight hundred metres, but because he ran a tactically bad race and got himself boxed in, he came second to Steve Ovett, his long-time rival. Five days later in the fifteen hundred metres final for which Ovett was very much the favourite, Coe turned the tables, taking the gold medal and breaking the world record in the process. In the eight hundred metres he had failed, in front of the world, and his pride had been deeply wounded. It would have been easy for him then to have lost confidence in himself as a champion, to have given up, to have found an excuse. But, rejecting the easy option, he took the experience of that eight hundred metres final, a goal he had worked towards for many years, and he used it as a catalyst to motivate him to win the fifteen hundred.

Failure can be an experience you identify with, or it can be a lesson you learn from. The choice is yours, and it will determine whether you perceive yourself as a loser or as a winner.

If you want to succeed, focus clearly on the outcome of the success you're striving for. Don't let past setbacks create mental blocks. Apply your mind and your skills to what you are doing. Banish all thoughts of failure.

Harry Houdini, the great American escapologist, at the height of his fame, issued this challenge: there was not a prison cell in America, he said, that could hold him. In due course he found himself in a cell that had a new kind of locking mechanism. Now, Houdini always carried about his body locksmith's tools, and so he set about trying to pick the lock, but without success. The hours passed, and he began to panic: the great Houdini had finally met his match: this lock was beyond his ability, his preparations must have been inadequate. And now in full view of the press he was going, for the first time, to fail spectacularly. He was just about ready to give up when in a last gesture of frustration he pulled on the door – only to have it open because the guards, in all the excitement, had failed to lock it.

So it is with facing our fear of failure. There is always another way of doing something; don't *assume* the solution is going to be hard to find, and don't overlook the obvious. Before you decide to give up on the apparently locked door, check the handle.

A small boy who loved cricket was given a new bat as a birthday present. Excitedly he dashed outside, shouting, 'I'm the best batsman in the whole world!', threw his ball high in the air, swung the bat and missed. Undeterred, he picked the ball up a second time and yelled defiantly, 'I'm the best batsman in the world!' This time he threw the ball much higher, kept his eye on it and took a bigger swing – but again he missed, pirouetting before falling to the ground. Now he was a bit bruised, but all the same he stood up a third time, threw the ball even higher, and took the biggest swing ever. This time he missed so completely that he lost hold of the bat and crashed to the ground so heavily that he grazed both knees. He sat up, looked at the bat, looked at the ball, then shouted excitedly, 'Hey, what do you know? I'm the greatest bowler in the world!'

You have to create a winning outlook and a strong self-belief; you have to turn those negative statements into positive statements. When you think to yourself, 'I really am old', see it in a positive light – you have a lot of experience and wisdom; instead of thinking, 'I'm not smart enough', say to yourself instead, 'I get on well with people, I'm enthusiastic about what I'm doing, and I'm reliable.'

When you look at the lives of people you admire, don't imagine yourself as being so different from them. Don't think it was easy for them – it wasn't. They will have had more or less the same number of hardships and setbacks that you will probably encounter. They didn't all have some kind of extraordinary natural talent, but what they did have was an extraordinary natural belief in what talent they had. And though they may have been unique in the way they ran their lives or set up their businesses, you too are unique. If you had the opportunity to meet one of your heroes, what qualities of yours would you like them to admire?

**Never give in – never, never, never give in.**
*Winston Churchill*

We've said before that successful people are individuals who get up one time more than they fall down. When you feel good about yourself, you take hiccups and even substantial obstacles in your stride. It's as though you are in harmony with the universe itself; nothing is a problem. But never lose sight of the fact that you *do* have a choice in how you feel about the hardships you encounter. And the choice you make will determine whether you persevere or whether you give up. By continuing to persevere you create a 'can do' image of yourself that becomes fixed in your subconscious; you develop a new set of behaviours and habits. This new set of behaviours and habits empowers you to endure and overcome the hardships that you may experience in the future.

When those who have succeeded in business talk of their early hardships and difficulties, they do not speak of experiences they wish they had never had. They talk of lessons learned, of character-building experiences that made them the people they are. And what they all had in common was the ability to persevere, to go through fear of failure and come out the other side.

> **Great works are performed not by strength but by perseverance.**
>
> *Samuel Johnson*

You can cover any distance, no matter how far, if you are prepared to persevere. Perseverance is not about pursuing the impossible – that is stupidity. As the old joke (attributed by some to Albert Einstein) goes, 'What is the difference between genius and stupidity?' The answer: 'I have learned in life that there is a limit to genius!'

Neither is perseverance exclusive to extraordinary individuals who have demonstrated superhuman feats of endurance; it is simply the determined resolve to work towards your chosen goal, come what may.

In a letter to his young son, G. Kingsley Ward, a Canadian businessman, wrote, 'No one I know has ever experienced a life without defeats, failures, disappointments and frustrations galore along the way; learning to overcome these times of agony is what separates the winners from the losers.'

## Focus on the prize, not the problem

I had a friend at university who played for the First XV rugby team. On one particular occasion there was an event that has subsequently become a source of much laughter whenever we retell the story. He was playing in a key qualifying game in a big intervarsity competition. The team was all psyched up, lined up, and ready to go – including my friend who was wearing a brand-new pair of rugby boots of which he was very proud. When the referee blew the whistle, everyone rushed forward to engage the opposition – except my friend who had stepped in a puddle and was standing there looking at his feet in disbelief, wailing, 'Oh no, my new boots – they're covered in mud!' For a moment his team was, in effect, one man short: he had taken his eye off the prize to dwell on his problem.

**Obstacles are those frightful things you see when you take your eyes off your goal**
*Henry Ford (1863–1947)*

When a setback occurs it's too easy to focus our energy on the injustice, the unfairness of it or simply be distracted by it. We should use that same focus and energy to find a solution, and move forward.

In 1961 John F. Kennedy declared his ambitious dream that America would put a man on the moon within the next ten years. At that time, the idea of being able to create the systems necessary to take three men to the moon, land them and bring them back, seemed almost to belong to the realms of science fiction; and yet on 20th July 1969 Neil Armstrong stepped on to the lunar surface. How was so much achieved so quickly? The fact is that the whole space race was driven by the Cold War, each nation competing with the other and seeking to demonstrate to the world its superior technology. It was this that concentrated the Americans on their goal, made them focus on the prize, and enabled them to overcome the countless problems that arose.

Focusing on the prize does not guarantee success, but it makes the journey towards it purposeful and confidence-building. The principal reason, I believe, why many people fail is because they lose sight of their initial dream. Their initial enthusiasm wanes because they start to focus on the consequences of failure. I have often met individuals who talk passionately to me about the business they are planning to set up. They are going to leave their safe employment in three months' time and go it alone. But as the starting date draws closer, they tell you more and more about the problems they are facing. These difficulties are no doubt real, but what's actually happening is that the fear factor has magnified and the consequences of imagined failure have become almost too awful to contemplate. And so, increasingly, whether they admit it or not, it's clear they've decided that inaction is the best policy.

Identify problems within your plan and let your subconscious mind solve them for you. Visualise yourself in your new company or office, or visualise the rewards and when the going gets tough return to these powerful visualisations of success in the future that you are creating. Once you have reached your goal, the journey you had to make to get there never seems so tough, because success has brought with it the habit of remembering strong positive memories of the experience, which your brain will now automatically store for use when you have to face future challenges.

The brain can be conditioned to focus on the positive and avoid remembering the negative. A sprinter focuses on the tape and on coming first. He doesn't focus on the opposition, because that would undermine his concentration. People who do well at auctions, on the other hand, look to successfully outbid others: they are not fearful of failing because they recognise that fear will harm their resolve. They may well have predetermined a cash ceiling above which they'll drop out. But they know that if they worry about being outbid their judgement may be affected, they may go over their limit and make a bad purchase. They cannot afford, literally, to focus on the problem rather than the prize. As the racing driver succintly expressed it when asked why he had not crashed replied 'I only concentrate on where I want to go.'

What happens when you have positive focus, pure and simple? Here's an example from my chosen sport – yes, golf again. It's an absolute joy to watch a young child putt for the first time. Children seem to have the most natural swings. Give them a four- or five-foot putt and they look at the hole, look at the ball, then swing the club and sink the putt – just as well as, if not better than, many an experienced golfer. They are complete naturals, utterly uninhibited by the fear of failure; they have no problems to focus on. They don't understand the mechanics of the golf swing or of the putting stroke; their minds are completely clear of negative thoughts or memories – of the junk that adults carry around with them. For children, putting is the most natural and easiest thing in the world.

As we grow older, though, we concentrate less on the desired outcome and more on the difficulties of getting there, trying to control things that are best left to the subconscious. And as long as you are preoccupied with problems you magnify them in your mind. As a golfer, you start hooding the blade, swinging across the line, lifting your head up, shortening your backswing – any or all of these in an attempt consciously to do it right.

So, when you close in on your target, whatever it may be, try to do so with the uncluttered and fearless approach of the child.

## Creative problem-solving

When we have a problem to solve we almost always resort to the same old habit of thinking, and so it's hardly surprising that we come up with the same old solution. And the same old solution may well be no solution at all to the issue in hand. What we have to do is develop a way of solving our problems creatively, allowing our imagination to play its natural role.

A high-rise office building was nearing completion. But when they came to put the lifts in they discovered they were too big for the shafts. Somewhere along the way imperial units had been used instead of metric. The engineers said it was technically impossible to widen the shafts; the lift company said it would take many months to make smaller lifts. Nobody seemed to know what to do, until a passing labourer suggested sticking the lifts on the outside of the building. It had never been tried before but they gave it a go, and it worked, and now external lifts are seen on buildings all around the world.

The point is that there is no one source of solutions.

When you do a crossword puzzle you follow a pattern of thought, but it's often this familiar pattern that you fall into that limits your ability to solve. Someone once said to me, 'If you want one way to solve a problem ask an expert, but if you want a hundred ask an idiot.'

We all tend to operate within the limits of our known abilities, instead of venturing outside them. Often people say, 'I'm not creative, I'm practical. I'm good with my hands but I'm not creative.' Put that to one side: do not be limited by a belief in your lack of imagination. Remember this above all else: ideas are currency; every project, every achievement, began as a creative spark in somebody's imagination.

You have an imagination that is capable of creating your solutions, so use it.

> **Ideas are like rabbits. You get a couple and learn how to handle them, and pretty soon you have a dozen.**
> *John Steinbeck (1902–68), American novelist*

How do you go about doing this? Start by writing the problem down – this will help you to clearly define what it is, to clearly see the parameters. Then, once you've identified the problem, write down as many ways of solving it as you can think of. They can be as far-fetched as you like – just let your mind empty itself of possible solutions, then leave it for a while. When you return to it a bit later your subconscious mind will have continued working on the difficulty; come back to it after several hours or even a day or two, and you'll be surprised at how quickly answers start to appear. Allowing your mind a free rein in this way will help to break the mould of your current habits of thought.

> **If you want a ten-mile-an-hour increase in train speed, you tinker with horsepower – double its speed, and you have to break out of conventional performance expectations.**
>
> *Jack Welch*

Everything created was first imagined. But in a normal corporate brainstorming session – and in all the companies I've worked for the call for a brainstorming session has been seen as a last-ditch attempt to solve a problem, or in some cases the first signs of panic about the future – I've found that one of three things generally happens:

1   Nothing. Everything stays the same, except that another brainstorming session is arranged for a later date.
2   The same solutions that have been heard in the past are re-presented by the people who have re-presented them systematically over the previous years.
3   A solution is adopted in which nobody really believes but which serves to keep the peace and move the project forward; voicing the feelings of most people present, someone mutters wearily, 'OK, that will do, let's go with that one.'

How often has that happened in your organisation? How often have you compromised on a solution that you know is wrong because the right solution eluded you?

I have found that a truly effective way of getting a creative session moving is to bring in a maverick thinker, somebody – perhaps from another area of your business – who has no real understanding of your operation, whose knowledge base is hopelessly deficient. But he possesses the great advantage of not having your habits of thinking; in other words, he isn't confined by your creative parameters, he doesn't live inside your box.

This person may well make suggestions that sound quite ridiculous or off the wall; but it's likely that some of the solutions he offers will contain the kernel of the right answer. He doesn't think in the same way that you think, because your patterns of thought have been shaped over the many years that you have spent in your particular corner of the industry. If the situation were to be reversed, you might well be able to do the same for his department, because his ideas and those of his colleagues are probably as much in need of a shake-up as yours are.

Ideas can come from anywhere. Whatever business you are in, you are first and foremost in the ideas business. When I worked at the BBC as a producer in the entertainment development unit our job was to look for and generate fresh ideas for television, from a variety of sources ranging from foreign broadcasters to members of the public. I must have read close on four thousand programme proposals in my years there, and the fact is I never saw a bad one. Certainly there were proposals which were so off the wall as to have no feasible place on a television schedule, but I always felt it was my responsibility to encourage anybody who wrote in. The strangest proposal I received was for a programme based on boxing and draughts. The idea was that two amateur boxers would box for three minutes, then play speed draughts for three minutes. The first person to submit or to lose at draughts was out! I remember my letter back:

Dear Sir,

Thank you very much for your proposal on boxing and draughts. I read it with interest and appreciate very much the thought and time that went into its construction. At the moment, due to the demands of the prime-time schedule, a programme of this type is not one we would be able to consider; however, thank you for letting us see your proposal, and should you have any other ideas you would like us to look at we would be delighted to see them.

Yours faithfully, etc.

The man wrote to me again, and though I couldn't take any of his ideas forward I always hoped my replies would encourage him to send me more – because, as I said earlier, there is no such thing as a good idea or a bad idea: there are simply ideas that can or that cannot be applied to a particular issue or at a particular time. It's rather like knowledge, in the sense that knowledge isn't power in itself – it's only applied knowledge that constitutes power. To tell someone that their ideas are no good is to stop them being creative and to deprive yourself of possible solutions to future problems.

For businesses to distinguish themselves from their competitors they have to be creative. They have to create unique selling points, to identify a niche in the market that they are best at, then pit their strength against their competitors'. All ideas originate in an individual's mind, and the more readily you can access this resource the more likely you are to gain the edge over your rivals. The creative process is one that we all have admission to. Ideas are currency: how much money is in *your* creative bank at the moment?

Being open to ideas from all sources pays enormous dividends. This clearly happened in the case of Toyota that I referred to earlier, whose forty-seven thousand employees generated 1.8 million suggestions in 1990. Companies that invite their staff to be involved in the creation of ideas that will impact on the business, or to identify problems and suggest solutions, benefit from a highly motivated, appreciative and loyal workforce.

> **The deepest principle of human nature is the craving to be appreciated.**
> *William James (1842–1910), American philosopher and psychologist*

Little things can make a big difference. Little suggestions can make the difference between things working and not working. Be open to your ability creatively to solve your problems. And when you're stumped ask others what they would do, how they would approach whatever it is that's impeding progress.

Companies often take their problems outside of the building and give them to other organisations – consultancies, troubleshooters – to solve. Now this may sound as if I'm trying to talk myself out of a job, but I strongly believe that if you put a group of individuals in a room and say, 'Don't come out until you have a solution to this problem', and tell them you believe in their ability to come up with one, you will frequently find not only the solution you need but one endorsed by your staff as well. And I can't emphasise too much how important it is that they feel appreciated and involved in the process.

When I was making television shows in small regional stations, I used to delight in watching the engineers solve unanticipated production difficulties. Never once did they say whatever it was couldn't be done. They would often go off for a while, then re-appear with some contraption they had designed on the spot to create just the effect we needed. As Scotty in *Star Trek* used to say, 'It's a long shot, Captain, but it might just work.' Trust your intuition, trust your long shots: they might just work.

## There's always another way

No matter how bleak things may appear, no matter how seemingly intractable the problem, never give up, never give in. There is *always* another way to skin that rabbit. To put it another way, when you feel you've reached the bottom there's only one way to go – up. What have you got to lose? Never live in fear that there is no solution. Never believe there is nothing to be done. You may need encouragement and practical help – but there is *always* a way through.

Think back to the Second World War, when many prisoners were interned in prisoner-of-war camps. What resources did they have? Very few, and yet by working together as a team they were able to devise so many ingenious ways of escaping: by digging tunnels, for instance, or by cobbling together elaborate disguises. They found a way.

See creative problem-solving as a tool. Have absolute faith in your ability and in the ability of friends and colleagues; be ready to exploit all the resources you can lay your hands on. *In The Very Very Rich and How They Got There*, Max Gunther singled out these two things as common to the subjects of his book:

1 Their shared philosophy: there is always a way, there is always a solution to this problem; it can be done.
2 Their practice of always prioritising and of working only on the things that truly mattered at the time.

Prioritising is the key to using your time effectively, and later we'll look at a simple way of creating daily, weekly and monthly priority lists. But the point to grasp now is that *there is always a solution*. Remember, many of the world's most important discoveries and achievements were made only after all had seemed lost – because people refused to give up.

But don't feel you should be looking for solutions only when things are not working. Start by seeking to improve your *modus operandi*, your current way of business, when things are going well. Some people say, 'If it ain't broke, don't fix it', and I agree with them. But I also think that, whatever your working methods, you should seek to improve on them.

Take IBM, for instance, who used to have the greatest research and development department in the computer industry, but also, unfortunately, the longest time lag in getting things from the research bench into the shop window. It was only being faced with record losses and the prospect of going out of business in the early 90s that forced them to change their procedure, to find a way of shortening the time lag so that they could not only compete with but outperform their competitors. In business, it may not be you who decides that things need fixing; usually, your competitors do it for you.

Commercial history is full of innovators whose ideas were ridiculed and ignored at the time only to come up trumps later. The creative process is all about respect for knowledge, and especially for imagination. Problems are puzzles to be solved, not handicaps to be overcome by. Never ridicule anyone's ideas – that's too easy to do and not in anyone's interest. If you don't like a particular suggestion, say something like 'I don't think this will work for us at the moment', but encourage the individual whose suggestion it is because one day he or she may come up with the gem that turns the business around.

It was rarely the case, I imagine, that the great inventors of the twentieth century woke up one morning with the exact solution to a problem complete in their minds. Trial and error were what brought their ideas to fruition. So when your plan is failing to get you to your destination, what do you do? Do you change your plan or do you change your destination? Champions always change their plan, fearlessly, with the confidence that they can do it; their destination remains the same.

# 9 The Winner Within

We were born with an inbuilt natural ability to succeed. In attempting to make sense of the world and overcome the obstacles along our path, our minds absorbed all the information they received. As children, we would set ourselves simple goals and we had the confidence to achieve them; and for the most part a pretty fearless bunch we were.

Have you ever noticed how naturally a very young child will climb a step-ladder in order to follow his father who's up there painting a window, or go up quite fearlessly to pet a dog in the park? But at the same time, young children are very impressionable. If a child is told by his mother that there is a monster under the bed all ready to grab his ankles if he gets up in the night, that child may well believe the statement to be true. What this does is to create a barrier in the child's mind. Fear has taken over. So what we condition children to believe in and what to expect are extremely important.

Is it *really* true that you can achieve any realistic goal you set yourself? Though such a claim may appear to be the stuff of fantasy, an insubstantial New Age mantra, I know that it isn't. Your success depends upon your *wanting* success; it depends on the goals you set yourself, the sacrifices you are willing to make, and the real benefits that you see this success bringing you.

> **Many persons have the wrong idea of what constitutes true happiness. It is not attained through self-gratification, but through fidelity to a worthy purpose.**
>
> *Helen Keller*

Certainly we all want the freedom that financial security gives, but hopefully we realise that money, of itself, does not bring happiness. A psychiatrist friend once observed to me that poor people go through life believing that money will make them happy, and this thought gives them hope; but his wealthy patients have realised that it doesn't, and frequently believe they have lost all hope.

To develop our winning potential, to maximise our chances of success, we need to be honest with ourselves and with others, to have high standards of personal integrity. Are your goals right for you – morally, ethically and spiritually? If you want to be successful, you cannot live a life at odds with the values you identify as crucial to that success. The happiness that comes from purely material success is often shallow, based perhaps on passing indulgence and ephemeral pleasure. By contrast, the success that comes from being truly happy is a wonderful feeling, a permanent lived-in-the moment experience.

Businessmen may argue that personal happiness is a wonderful thing but that in the corporate world business is business. It's about quality, service, product, aftersales and distribution. They need to make a profit; that is the bottom line, and without it they are simply not in business. But in their pursuit of profit companies can lose sight of exactly who is delivering the quality, the products and the after-sales. Too often, the 'internal excellence' programmes that many companies implement focus on delivering the bottom line and not on developing the people who deliver.

Corporate success demands integrity, ethnical standards and quantifiable achievements, and companies that hold these core values tend to hold on to their staff.

> **Take away my people but leave my factory and soon grass will be growing on the shop floor; however, take away my factory and leave me my people, and we will build another business.**
> *Andrew Carnegie (1835–1919), Scottish steel magnate and philanthropist*

The Natural Born Winners approach to success is not a quick-fix solution but a structured programme that will help you on that journey from where you are now to where you want to be in the future. And it will do so without compromising your standards – indeed, it may well confirm and consolidate them. Your integrity is a quality you can only lose once – so don't compromise it.

An American high-school coach always called his students, 'Champ'. When asked why, he said it was because he wanted them all to go through life thinking of themselves as champions. To create the future that you want, think of yourself as a champion. Just as you must take responsibility for your physical well-being by following a healthy diet and exercise programme, so to achieve a successful mind-set you have to train your mind. And just as exercise and diet will *condition* your body, it is equally within your grasp to develop a permanent sense of harmony and well-being.

We grow up with many natural talents, but such is our longing for social acceptance within our peer group that, in order to fit in, we hide them. Rediscover, develop and use those talents.

## Your motivation

Much has been written on motivation, but what exactly is it? The word 'motivation' brings to mind *motive* and *action* – when you are seeking to achieve something you *move* towards your objective. But what *is* your motive? Is yours internal or external, or both? Whatever it is, it's the force that will drive you on.

Identify what motivates you; your internal motive will be your determination to change. Internal motivation can be very powerful, if it is a deep-felt commitment. A group of people decide to give up alcohol for the month of January: the ones who do it successfully once can do it every year, because they are internally committed to doing so. External motivation is equally powerful: little is more likely to stop you drinking than being told by the doctor that your liver will pack up if you don't.

We can motivate ourselves to want an object – a new car, for instance. You could also cut out a picture of the car, stick it on the wall above your desk and every day look at it and visualise owning it. Your determination to own it would be the internal motivator; the picture of the car, the external one.

**We don't remember days; we remember moments.**
*Cesare Pavese (1908–50), Italian novelist and poet*

Our motivators vary according to our goal. Early man was driven by a need for food and shelter, for without food he would have starved and without shelter he would have been exposed to danger and the elements. For the fortunate majority in our society starvation and exposure are almost non-existent, and so in the modern world we are motivated by other triggers: we seek financial security, to provide for our families and to guard our personal well being.

What is your trigger?

I remember being in a mini-cab in London driven by a Ghanaian. On his dashboard was a picture of three small children. I asked him if they were his, he said with great pride that they were and that he was soon hoping they would be able to come and join him in England. I asked him how he enjoyed being a mini-cab driver. It was good, he said, because he earned money from it; he was by profession a qualified engineer but could get no engineering work over here, so he kept the picture of his children there to remind him constantly of why he was driving the cab twelve hours a day, seven days a week.

For the cab-driver, this was a powerful trigger. And you too have triggers that you need to identify in order to help motivate yourself. Many goal-setting techniques use pictures and other images as motivators, encouraging you to construct a clear vision of the future you want – the house, the car, the holiday or whatever it may be. Consolidating this vision involves continually referring back to the image as well as repeating daily positive affirmations that reinforce the subconscious emotional memory.

Setbacks and crises can be great motivators. Many people who lose their jobs later say it was the best thing that ever happened to them. It forced them to focus on what things they really wanted to do with the rest of their lives; it motivated them away from their comfort zone. But motivation without a firm and resolved faith in our ability to succeed will never be truly effective. Also, when motivation is purely personal or self-interested it is much more difficult to keep it going day by day than when it is employed in the service of others. When the greater good is at issue, then motivation is more powerful because it is supported by values.

In business, although people may initially be motivated by money or perhaps by power or position, these do not necessarily remain the most important triggers. An American company, Glenn Tobe & Associates, conducted a survey in which they asked supervisors to rank the importance of ten motivators for their employees. They they asked the employees to rank the same list in order of what they most wanted from their supervisors.

The results are shown on the following page.

Time and time again companies pay lip-service to the importance of appreciation and involvement, and yet they spend so much energy motivating their staff exclusively through incentive schemes, loyalty packages and money. They're missing the point. Of course money is a motivator, but not the only one. A word of praise is priceless.

A study done in Massachusetts into the causes of heart disease asked participants two questions: 'Are you

| *Supervisors* | *Employees* |
|---|---|
| 1 Good wages | 1 **Appreciation** |
| 2 Job security | 2 **Feeling 'in' on things** |
| 3 Promotional opportunities | 3 **Understanding attitude** |
| 4 Good working conditions | 4 Job security |
| 5 Interesting work | 5 Good wages |
| 6 Loyalty from management | 6 Interesting work |
| 7 Tactful discipline | 7 Promotional opportunities |
| 8 **Appreciation** | 8 Loyalty from management |
| 9 **Understanding attitude** | 9 Good working conditions |
| 10 **Feeling 'in' on things** | 10 Tactful discipline |

happy?' and 'Do you love your work?' The results showed that those who answered yes to both were statistically less likely to get heart disease. Another American study, by Srully Blotwick in 1982, had followed over twenty years fifteen hundred people, divided into two groups. Group A, 83 per cent of the total, comprised those who had chosen their particular career with a view to making as much money as possible so that they could do their own thing in their spare time. To group B, the remaining 17 per cent, money was secondary: they had gone for careers for which they felt a passion. After the data was analysed it produced a startling discovery: after twenty years 101 of the 1,500 had become millionaires. Of the millionaires all but 100 of the 101 were from Group B, the group that had chosen to pursue what they loved.

Your core values and your passion for what you are doing are the strongest motivators when it comes to how you act, think and work.

What is *your* passion? Identify it and get it to work for you. The pursuit of your personal success won't necessarily bring with it great riches; but it frequently happens that when we achieve personal success, we automatically create wealth for ourselves.

## Your core values

Many companies point with obvious pride to their 'mission statements' (see p. 136), which extol the supreme values of the organisation and their (optimistic) vision of the future. What are *your* supreme values?

Are you always fair, honest, kind, humble, helpful, trustworthy, courageous? If asked, we would all probably say, yes, more or less, to most of these questions. Most of us see ourselves as all right, as being in what I call the OK zone. But I don't think the OK zone is where we really want to be, because it's where we are when our behaviour doesn't *really* match up with our core values. How is your honesty? 'It's OK.' How is your fairness? 'It's OK.' But OK isn't good enough, is it? We should always be striving towards the fantastic zone and aiming to do and to be our best.

But if your values are at odds with your goal, success will almost certainly elude you – or if it doesn't elude you it won't last long because it will be built on shallow foundations. Except in a life-and-death situation, would you steal, would you make a false claim, would you lie in order to win a contract? We have all at some time told white lies so as to spare people's feelings, or rewritten our CVs to fiction-prize winning standard. And we've done it and fully justified it because we've believed the end justifies the means. But we've also known, at heart, that no amount of justification could make it right.

Strive to create for yourself an ethical standard of which you can be proud and that others will hold up as an example of personal excellence. As the saying goes: 'If you are suffering from lack of self-worth, perhaps you are not doing anything worth while.'

I am not talking about being a goody-goody, a saintly figure far removed from the common run, but I *am* talking about personal integrity. In the pursuit of personal and professional success it *is* important that you do the right thing. That you *don't* cheat, steal or lie, even in ways that may be regarded as socially acceptable or even justifiable. There can be few of us who haven't at one time or other said things like 'Well, everyone does it', 'The company can afford it', or 'Someone did the same thing to me'. But when you corrupt your ethical standards in such ways, even just a little bit, a rot can quickly set in.

Racquetball player Ruben Gonzales got through to the final in his first professional tournament where he was playing against the defending champion. In the last moment of the match he hit a shot down the line that was called 'in' by both judge and line judge. He had won his first pro tournament, it seemed. But Gonzales lost no time in telling them that the shot had actually gone out and they'd misread it, and he asked for it to be played again. It was, and he lost the tournament. He was asked later why, at such an auspicious moment, he had challenged the judges' decision and allowed his opponent back in. He answered simply that it was because he knew the ball was out, and he could not have allowed himself to claim victory. His integrity was not for sale.

Think about what your core values are. Identify them and strive to live them every day.

## Responsibility

We all make mistakes, and we all have a personal responsibility to ourselves, to the people we interact with and to the world at large. How we deal with our mistakes can crucially affect the outcome of our future behaviour. Too many of us blame others for our mistakes. No matter how we look at it, when things go wrong we all have a personal responsibility for which no one else is account-able. We may say, 'The reason I'm like I am is because when I was little I didn't get any love', or 'It's not my fault I'm late – I've always been late' – acknowledging the problem but accepting no responsibility. But we must accept in the end that we are the person we *choose* to be.

Remember that the one thing in your life you have total control over is your attitude, and we've seen that you can learn new perspectives that will improve it. It's not easy, changing a lifetime's habits – but rest assured that if you can imagine it, you can do it. And accept your failures along the way. I have said many times how vital it is that you learn not to identify yourself with failure but see it as a learning experience.

Live your own life. Don't waste time comparing yourself with others – you may be unaware of how little you know their situations or their aims in life. When I was at the Royal Marsden Hospital I was told never to discuss my case with anyone else because they might well offer me information or opinions that bore no relationship to my case, but that might nonetheless affect my feelings about my illness in unhelpful ways. Don't judge others, either. You may know next to nothing of their situation and circumstances.

I believe that management has a responsibility to its staff to trust and encourage them, to have faith in their intuition and creativity, to believe in their capacity to solve problems. It is the company's responsibility to help their staff develop within the business. But staff must repay this trust; they must accept *their* responsibility to do the very best job they can, be willing to take their ideas to management, to become involved, to convince management that they are worthy of their trust.

Above all, you are responsible for how you think and act, and this includes how you respond to failure. If, for instance, you feel that someone is deliberately holding you back at work, then talk to them or talk to someone who can help you. Remember to ask, ask, ask. It may be just a question of misunderstanding, or maybe you are not ready for the promotion – or maybe you are working for the wrong company!

Think of the consequences if you do nothing. When you have the opportunity to effect positive change, to fail to do so is a terrible waste of resource.

# Perception

We have all witnessed 'magic', whether on the stage or on television. A certain trick leaves us amazed at what has happened – we've just witnessed something that's impossible! Of course, it was all to do with what we *saw*, as opposed to what was actually happening. Quite simply, we were the subject of misdirection or illusion.

**We do not see things as they are. We see them as we are.**

*The Talmud*

What you see, hear and believe dictates how you respond and act. Life experience and personal belief all shape your perceptions of the world, yourself and your future. If you want to change the way you see the world and act in it, you must let go of your negative perceptions and beliefs and create a new and honest vision of your future. When someone says, 'I wish I could change my nose, because the one I've got is too big', they believe without any doubt that it's their nose that's holding them back; and this conviction affects the way they feel about themselves, becomes the reason for much unhappiness and lack of fulfilment.

Examine the way you think, examine your most deeply held beliefs. Ask yourself whether these perceptions are truthful and honest or no more than illusions that you have created.

# Purpose

**Joy is not in things, it is in us.**
*Richard Wagner (1813–83), German composer*

Without a sense of meaning we are lost. The pursuit of happiness without a purpose is impossible, because the mind needs to identify clearly with a goal. Given that our happiness is not going to reside solely in the acquisition of material goods, power, rank or position, we must find a purpose that transcends these things. And I'm not suggesting that this necessarily involves some complex spiritual or philosophical quest. True winners are those who realise their true potential, and they do so by consciously having found goals with purpose and meaning. We witness the opposite end of the spectrum in people who pursue temporary oblivion through drink or drugs in order to bring brief relief to lives that have *no* meaning or purpose.

Years ago a friend told me of a long period when he had been in the depths of depression, of an existential anxiety. Questions to do with the purpose and meaning of life haunted him, and he could find no answers that gave him any comfort. Though brought up a Christian, he was not religious; he had seen too much religious hypocrisy, and had chosen not to have any beliefs. Having been driven to near-desperation by his feelings of helplessness and hopelessness, he eventually realised one day that his purpose in life was simply to do his best, to leave the world a better place than he had found it and to help as many people along the way as he safely could. It seemed too cute a solution to me, too simple, but since it was clearly helping him I questioned it no further.

I didn't recognise it until much later, but the fact was that he had indeed found a purpose. He had discovered the very core values that brought everything else into perspective. For him these values were to do with doing his best in the service of others, and the discovery released him from his painful anxiety, his sense of worthlessness, his paralysing lack of direction. I believe our lives are journeys of self-discovery. Ultimately the values and true success that we seek are realised at a spiritual level when we reach the understanding that success, joy and happiness lie not in things, places or people, but within ourselves. Nevertheless, sometimes being nice for the sake of it has its own rewards, whatever you believe.

When you are ninety-six years old and your parachute fails on your sky-diving course somewhere over the Nevada Desert, I very much doubt this book is going to flash through your mind. What I do believe is that you'll remember those moments in your life when you were fully involved, fully belonging and fully appreciated, those moments when you gave yourself completely to whatever it was you were doing. You will see those times for what they were – times when you were fully alive.

> **You will find, as you look back upon life, that the moments that stand out are the moments when you have done things for others.**
> *Henry Drummond (1851–97), theologian*

## Appreciation

Do you appreciate yourself? Do you often tell yourself, 'Well done!' Or are you always finding fault with yourself? People who fail to realise their goals, or who have a history of failure, rarely appreciate their own abilities; they are forever finding fault and looking for reasons why they cannot succeed.

So it is important that every time you accomplish even a small step towards your goal, you praise your effort. Winners may often be modest and unassuming, but they have confidence in themselves. When a training session is finished they tell themselves very clearly, 'Well done, that was good!' And what they are doing is to create a powerful memory of each small achievement.

Appreciation is a great motivator – as you'll know, when you don't get it. Time and again we hear of its importance at work. But how often has your boss failed to say thank you, even when you've worked hard and late, perhaps over the weekend, in order to meet a deadline? Little is more demoralising than our best efforts going unappreciated.

And of course, the opposite is equally true. I remember being on a bus once, and as one of the passengers came to get off he turned to the driver and said, 'Thanks for the ride.' The driver seemed momentarily taken aback, but then he smiled and said, 'Hey, it's my job, but thanks.' The passenger, I guess, had simply developed a habit of thanking people who helped him or came into his life in some other way. Think of the times when you've been driving and you've pulled over to the side of the road to let another vehicle through a narrow stretch, and as he passes the other driver doesn't wave, or toot the horn, or smile – he just passes on. How do you feel about that? I always think they could at least have acknowledged me, recognised my existence. On the other hand, when someone does say thanks, the pulling over never seems such an inconvenience, and you feel a little surge of pleasure.

> **It is one of the most beautiful compensations of life that no man can sincerely try to help another without helping himself.**
>
> *Ralph Waldo Emerson*

When you praise somebody, show appreciation of their efforts – even in very small ways such as by expressing gratitude or showing courtesy – you both benefit. They appreciate your thanks, and you feel good about making somebody realise they are appreciated. But important as it is to appreciate others, above all don't forget yourself. It is by acknowledging your own little successes along the way that your confidence will grow. And as your confidence grows, so your successes will multiply – a powerful, positive and self-fulfilling process will be set in train.

Many people, for many different reasons, have low self-esteem. They believe they are unlovable, unworthy. Feelings of low self-worth will handicap your ability to develop – you have to find strategies to overcome them.

One way to start is by writing out a list of the things in your life that you are grateful for. This will help you to focus on the good in your life, no matter how trivial the things on your list may seem. They will help you to identify with the positive; they will help you to see yourself as a person capable of achievement and enjoyment. Your list may start with just one thing or several: 'I appreciate the sunshine, I appreciate my friends, I appreciate my love of books, I appreciate having a regular income . . .'

Make your list as short or as long as you like, and return to it and add to it whenever you wish. You will have started to create feelings of gratitude, which will gradually transform into feelings of hopefulness and self-worth.

## What would you do differently if you had a second chance?

Have you ever fantasised about what you would do differently if you were eighteen all over again, but had your current wisdom and experience? I am sure there are so many things we would do differently, with hindsight.

Here is a simple exercise that I do frequently as part of the Natural Born Winner programme.

Look at one aspect of your life that you would like to change. It might be starting your own business, it might be moving to the country, it might be eating more healthily, it might be about having a more balanced and loving relationship with your partner. Just stop for a moment and identify one aspect of your life that you would like to change. Sit quietly; think about your current situation; and then visualise yourself ten years hence, having changed not one bit, exactly the same as you are now. See yourself ten years older, and feel your frustration and anger at your lack of progress. Then, while visualising that scene ask yourself, as if you were now ten years into the future, 'If I could go back ten years and have this chance again, what changes would I make, what would I do? Now stop the visualisation, and realise that you are now living in that day: *the day that you have the chance to change the future.*

The changes you want to make so as to avoid the future you don't want can be made now: they are completely within your control. Start them now, immediately. Do it differently. Do it now.

> **If I had my life to live over again, I'd try to make more mistakes next time. I would relax. I'd be sillier than I have been on this trip. I would climb more mountains, swim more rivers and watch more sunsets. I would have more actual troubles and fewer imaginary ones. Oh, I've had my moments, and if I had to do it all over again I'd have more of them. In fact I'd try to have nothing else, just moments, one after another . . . I would pick more flowers.**
>
> *Nadine Stair (aged eighty-nine)*

Remember, you will never have today again. Time is the one thing we all have an equal share of. It doesn't matter whether you are Bill Gates or the Queen, or the guy selling newspapers on the street corner. We all have sixty seconds to each minute, sixty minutes to each hour. Don't waste this time – once gone, it never comes back! Put a time-frame on every task you want to achieve. With a time-frame, it's so much easier to meet your deadline. Do we often forget Christmas Day? No. Because it's a date that has been set for us.

One thing is for sure: we can't go back and change the past. But, as I mentioned earlier, many of us carry its baggage around and use the past to excuse our present condition or to anticipate future failure. But let's be quite clear – though we can't change the past, we *can* let go of it. We can choose to determine our future. And the best place to start is by living in the present, because that's the bit you control.

There was once a handsome young king who, for all his power and fortune, was bothered by two questions that he continually asked himself: 'What will be the most important time in my life?' and 'Who will be the most important person in my life?' So he issued a challenge to the philosophers of the world, saying that whoever successfully answered these two questions for him would share his wealth. They came from all over the country and beyond, but none had the answer the king was seeking. Then somebody told him of a wise man who lived many days' journey away in the mountains. At once, the king set off.

Arriving at the foot of the mountain where the wise man lived, he disguised himself as a peasant. When he reached the wise man's simple hut, he found him sitting cross-legged on the ground, digging. 'I hear you are a wise man and can answer everything,' he said. 'Can you tell me who is going to be the most important person in my life and what will be the most important time?' 'Help me dig some potatoes,' the old man said. 'Take them down to the river and wash them. I'll boil some water and you can share some soup with me.'

Thinking this was a test, the king did as he was asked. He stayed with the old man for several days hoping that his questions would be answered, but no answers were forthcoming.

So now he pulled out his royal seal, identified himself as the king and denounced the old man as a fraud. He spoke of his anger at wasting days of his life with him. 'I answered your questions when we first met,' the old man replied, 'but you didn't understand my answers.' 'What do you mean?' said the king. 'I made you welcome when you arrived,' the old man went on, 'and I shared my home with you. You should know that the past is gone and the future doesn't exist – the most important time in your life is now, and the most important person in your life is the person you are with now because he is the one with whom you are sharing and experiencing life.'

> There are two things to aim at in life: first, to get what you want and, after that, to enjoy it. Only the wisest of mankind achieve the second.
>
> *Logan Pearsall Smith (1865–1946),*
> *American essayist and critic*

## Laugh more

After being released from the high-dependency unit at the Royal Marsden Hospital, I was returned to a small four-bed room. Because of some post-operative discomfort I wasn't sleeping very well and couldn't concentrate on books or magazines. At one point I noticed that two of the other patients in the unit were dozing, but the third was watching the TV. So I put on my headset and idly started to watch too. It turned out to be a very funny programme and painful though it was, I couldn't stop myself laughing. Every time I laughed, the stitches in my abdomen tugged and I yelled out – but I just couldn't stop myself laughing. It was a case of a moment's laughter followed by a moment's agony. I looked across at the other man who was watching, and he was laughing as well; both our beds were silently shaking. At that moment I came alive again to the wonderful power of laughter: I started for the first time to truly feel well again on the inside.

> The most wasted of all days is that during which one has not laughed.
>
> *Nicolas Chamfort (1741–94), French moralist and*
> *essayist*

Laugh frequently and laugh often is good advice; and if you can't find anything to laugh about, you may be taking *everything* too seriously – don't. Relax and be open to those moments of spontaneous joy. Laughing enhances our sense of well-being. Take a lesson from the American who, diagnosed with cancer, booked himself into a hotel, hired a projector and a bunch of his favourite comedy films, and laughed himself back to health.

Do try to see the funny side of things. Often, it's only in retrospect that we can see something that seemed deadly serious at the time as actually quite comical. How much better to be able to relax enough to find the humour in the moment. Soldiers, doctors and people who work in the emergency services use black humour so as to diffuse the distress of the tragedies that they regularly encounter. 'I didn't know whether to laugh or cry' is something we quite often say. If you have a choice of laughing or crying, it's usually better to laugh.

Cheer yourself up! Do you have any favourite films? I do, and sometimes I'll watch them more than once in the course of a year, maybe just playing a favourite scene. When you smile you automatically increase your feelings of well-being; your mind is triggered by the act of smiling to remember happy memories. America has laughter consultants who work exclusively in the workplace, helping companies to lighten up and have fun. For instance, they'll suggest holding Elvis look-alike days and bad-dressing days: part of their task is to impress on management the beneficial effects of their staff having fun.

Remember what one American comic said to his son on his deathbed: 'You know, I figure if you go through life making at least one person laugh, every day, you will have made a pretty good account of yourself.' Given the choice of being deadly serious throughout life or laughing at its absurdities, I know what I would choose – every time.

**To laugh often and much, to win the respect of intelligent people and the affection of children; to earn the appreciation of honest critics and endure**

the betrayal of false friends; to appreciate beauty;
to find the best in others; to leave the world a bit
better, whether by a healthy child, a garden patch
or a redeemed social condition; to know even one
life has breathed easier because you have lived.
This is to have succeeded.

*Ralph Waldo Emerson*

Laughter can be a physical expression of joy and well-being, or just a response to something funny. Look for funny moments in your life, look for things that make you laugh. When you get together with your friends, what stories do you tell each other? Often you find at reunions, say, that you tend to talk about past shared experiences, but more often you recall those moments that made you laugh. And when you laugh, you are taken out of yourself; it's a wonderful feeling.

Never underestimate the power of laughter in your life. Seek it, enjoy it, develop it, be healed by it.

Important as it is to laugh at things in life, learn as well to laugh at yourself. Never take yourself too seriously. If you make a silly mistake, laugh at the absurdity of it and move forward. Don't feel embarrassed, anxious or ashamed: laugh at yourself and learn the lesson. No other species has a sense of humour or the ability to benefit from laughter. Our ability to share in its transforming power did not develop by chance; its purpose may not be clear, but it sure is fun. Make the best of it.

# 10 New Beginnings

As I've said before, if you do what you've always done you'll get what you've always got. It follows that if you are not successful, if your life is not where you want it to be, then it's an absolute certainty that nothing is going to change until you determine to *make* it change – it's that simple, that's the bad news.

The good news is that you have the capacity to change whenever you want to. Don't think of yourself as an old dog who can't learn new tricks. Don't think of yourself as someone so embedded in old patterns that it would be impossible for you to transform yourself. It's never too late to make a change in your life. It really doesn't matter what age you are. So forget that excuse, for a start.

You want to be a success; you want to achieve your personal goals. This chapter will show you how to create and implement a personal blueprint, a life-planner that you can use to achieve both professional and personal success. A word of warning, though: remember that it is you alone who have to do it. So all the personal-development and self-help books, all the inspirational audio- and video tapes in the world, all the seminars you may attend and all the encouraging words from friends – none of this will count for a jot if *you* do not commit to making it happen.

So, before you set out to change the world, learn first to change yourself. Change is a difficult thing to achieve. It's no coincidence that we talk of habits being 'broken', because breaking a habit is often a painful process, and we naturally tend to resist pain. All the same, hard though it may be, habits *can* be broken; and it's when you successfully break one that's been hindering you that you start to believe in success.

Resolve to persist until your goal is realised. It's said, and I know from experience, that in a marathon the last mile is the longest. You never get to find that out until you have run the first twenty-five and a half, of course. But the point is that you are capable of achieving so much more than you currently believe; and so, in order to make this programme work for you, you must get away from a self-image that restricts your personal growth. See yourself as the success you were born equipped to become. Understand that all change begins with a change in attitude and a change in thinking. Whatever your personal history you can, if you determine to, break through those inhibiting beliefs.

> **The greatest discovery of my generation is that a human being can alter his life by altering the attitude of his mind.**
>
> *William James*

Whatever you can visualise powerfully and believe in absolutely, you can achieve. It takes proper planning, persistence and unwavering confidence. But once you have all of these you are bound to reach your goal.

'Today is the first day of the rest of your life.' Cliché though this may be, it is nonetheless true. You might equally say that yesterday was the last day of your old life. What has gone before has shaped the person you are. If you don't like that person, determine today that you are going to change. Don't think about what might go wrong.

If you need more encouragement, consider these examples. In its first year of business Coca-Cola sold only four hundred bottles. Mr Gillette, the man who created disposable razor blades, was at first ridiculed by many companies who said his project was doomed to failure; in his first year of business he sold just fifty-seven of his blades. David Hartman, a young American who went blind at the age of eight, became at twenty-seven the first blind person to complete medical school. Beethoven was totally deaf when he wrote his famous Ninth Symphony. The inventor of the 'Post-it' note persisted with his idea even after the marketing campaign had been deemed a total failure and his investors had lost confidence in the product.

'Success follows your last failure', so the saying goes; and none of these people knew when their last failure was going to be, but they persevered, all the same. Every success has its price: to some it comes easily, for others it takes a great deal of effort; but the common factors, as I've said before, are complete belief, dedication and persistence. So with that thought at the front of your mind let's go on now to consider the creation and development of your future success.

## You Ltd

There is a professor at a university in America who says to all of his new students on their first day: 'If I could buy you for what you think you are worth and sell you for what I *know* you are worth, I'd be a millionaire.'

Too many people undervalue themselves. They have a low opinion of their abilities and of their potential. But if you don't value yourself, who will? In the business world, companies that attract investors are valued for their potential, not simply for their basic financial assets. Equally, you should value yourself on your potential. Think of yourself in terms of what you could achieve, not in terms of what you've done already. You'll be amazed.

Think of yourself as a business, as a good investment for the future! Let's call this business You Ltd. Is it a progressive business or is it risk-averse? What are its resources and morale like? How is it going to grow one day to become You plc?

In large companies there are different departments

with diverse functions – research, marketing, sales, distribution, manufacturing, finance, human resources and so on. They are all working towards the success of the organisation of which they are part. They are meant to complement each other, to work in harmony; if they don't there will be problems. Businesses refer to these departments as divisions or silos. They may operate independently of each other, but if they are not singing from the same hymn sheet difficulties, often catastrophic ones, can arise.

For example, a sales department promises to deliver a consignment of new products to a major client. The research department has told the client that the product will be ready by a certain date. But no one has told the manufacturing department, and they can't gear themselves up to handle the order because the finance department isn't ready to release the funds that they thought were available. Now the budget is going up the spout because money is having to come from another source, in this case from the distribution department. Lack of communication has thus resulted in a giant headache for the company, and a loss of external confidence and internal morale, as well as of money.

Just as organisations are made up of departments, so are you: you have your own departments, distinct aspects of yourself, that go into making you the person you are, and it's important that, just like the departments in a company, these should be working in harmony. No individual is greater than his department; no department is greater than the company. Similarly, no one aspect of your life is more important than the other aspects. There is a saying in sport that a champion team can beat a team of champions any time.

To be truly happy and successful you need to be operating as efficiently as a well run business. So let's substitute the roles of departments, and replace them with the individual aspects of your life which need to be performing at their peak. I have identified seven: *self*, *health, attitude, relationships, spirit, career* and *wealth*. We shall look at these in more detail shortly, but first let's have a status report on You Ltd. How is it doing?

What's your answer? It is just 'OK'? Well, if so, I don't think that's good enough. You deserve to be functioning better than OK. You weren't born to be just 'OK' – you were born to be great.

What does your current life chart look like?

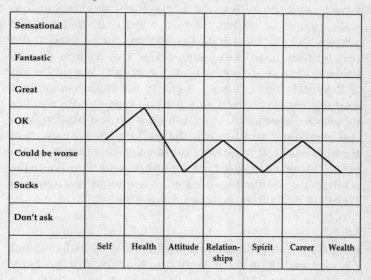

| | Self | Health | Attitude | Relation-ships | Spirit | Career | Wealth |
|---|---|---|---|---|---|---|---|
| Sensational | | | | | | | |
| Fantastic | | | | | | | |
| Great | | | | | | | |
| OK | | | | | | | |
| Could be worse | | | | | | | |
| Sucks | | | | | | | |
| Don't ask | | | | | | | |

If You Ltd is doing merely OK, then I don't think I want to invest in it. I want your company to be doing great. I want your company to be kickin' ass, I want to back a winner. If your life chart indicates that the main aspects of your life are just OK or worse, then you need to get your life plan on track and operating at a level that will guarantee success.

## Your seven aspects

When I began creating the Natural Born Winners

development programme, I identified seven aspects of my own life that I believed needed to be working at a level beyond OK if I was to stay on track. You may identify in your own life aspects that are important to you but that I have not listed here. Feel free to include them in your life chart. But I do believe these seven are essential, and I would advise you not to neglect any of them.

The bottom axis of your chart contains your seven aspects, and the left-hand axis has the scale. Look at that scale for a moment. At the mid-point I've written 'OK'; below it, 'Could be worse'; below that, 'Sucks'; and at the very bottom, 'Don't ask.' Above 'OK' I've written 'Good'; above that, 'Great'; above that, 'Fantastic'; and at the top of the scale, 'Sensational'. A pretty subjective scale, you may say. So it is. And I suggest you make yours equally subjective – not just 1 to 10, which is far too precise. Feel free to create your own, one that reflects the way you feel about yourself. If 'Fantastic' is your top line, I want you to be operating at Fantastic for the rest of your life – Fantastic is what you should be aiming for – and what you deserve!

Let's now look at those seven aspects.

## Self

How do you feel about yourself? How do you feel about your future? Do you feel confident that you can meet any challenge face on? How is your self-image – are you comfortable with it? Do you like it? Do you *like* who you are? Are you proud of yourself? Are there aspects of your behaviour that you're ashamed of? How do you look? When you look in the mirror in the morning, do you like what you see?

I remember once after a celebration that had gone on rather late, waking up the next morning and catching a reflection of myself in the mirror. I did a double take, looked again, then said out loud, 'Dad!' It had finally dawned on me that I was getting older, that I was no longer the fresh-faced youth I imagined myself to be. For a time I felt a bit gloomy about it, but in due course I realised it was nothing to be worried about. It was just part of the process of life.

How are you ageing? Are you ageing well, or is it something you are not comfortable with? Do you like your own company? How near are you to 'fantastic'?

*Health*

By health I mean both your physical and your mental well-being. Are you taking care of yourself? Are you surprised at the way some people treat their bodies? The way they use food and drink and other substances without thinking of the consequences. And their ability to neglect the idea of exercise altogether!

I love watching people on a Sunday washing their cars, checking the oil and the battery, making sure that everything is working just right. They do all this because they can put a value on the car, it's worth a fixed sum of money – they really love that car. But it sometimes seems as if they don't' value half as much that wonderfully sophisticated and complex piece of organic engineering, the like of which it is so far beyond our ability to replicate – the human body.

Are you looking after *your* body? And if not, why not? Your health should be a priority. Physically fit people cope with stress much better than the unfit. Make an appointment with your GP for a medical examination; then put together a well-being programme to get yourself fit.

*Diet*

Pay attention to your diet. 'You are what you eat', the saying goes. There is so much information available on nutrition in bookshops and libraries: on which foods to combine with which, on what constitutes a good diet, whether generally or specifically – high-protein, low-fat, and so on. Bear in mind in particular that our bodies are perfectly adapted to the foodstuffs available in nature, and try to eat more organic foods. I enjoy the occasional hamburger and fries as much as the next person – but all things in moderation! Don't abuse your body by filling it with junk.

*Exercise* Are you taking *any* exercise? Even the smallest amount will impact positively on your life. Studies of seventy-year-old men who started doing simple weight-training have shown a decrease in blood pressure and an increase in muscle tone. You are never too old to exercise. Even if for you it means merely walking for five minutes longer or occasionally taking the stairs instead of the elevator, still do it.

A very important part of your health is relaxation – stress management. Everyone feels stressed from time to time: the key is knowing how to manage it. We need to learn to relax in a natural, healthy way that is not dependent on cigarettes, alcohol or other substances.

How much time do you set aside for physical relaxation? I meditate in the morning and in the evening. Sometimes I do it only for five minutes, sometimes for twenty, but the benefit to my life is immeasurable. Though I still experience stress, I don't suffer its effects anything like as much as I used to. Yes, there are times when everything seems to be happening at once, but I am able to stay calm even though my mind may be racing. My body doesn't follow suit because I have learned to keep it relaxed. I will share my technique with you shortly, but there are many methods available via tapes, books and classes. Look into them and then adopt the one that best suits you.

## Attitude

Is your attitude positive or is it negative? Are you an optimist or a pessimist? Do you expect the worst and hope for the best?

Your attitude is the one thing you can immediately change. Of course, you won't instantly shed your old patterns of thinking and behaving, but you'll discover that by controlling your attitude, you can genuinely affect the way you respond to situations. Determine that it will be a positive attitude, that you won't let yourself be frustrated or angered by things that got to you before. Your attitude determines not only how you see the world, but ultimately how the world sees you. Get your attitude right, and everything else will become easier. You are looking not for OK – you're striving for fantastic!

*Relationships*

I'm talking about relationships in the sense of everyone you interact with – your family and loved ones, your work colleagues, friends, associates – even strangers you come into contact with in the course of a day and may never see again. Whoever you meet you have a relationship with.

How do you relate to them and how do you allow them to relate to you? I rather like this old aphorism: 'Always judge a person by the way they treat another person who can be of no use to them.'

What is your relationship within a team? How do you perceive the team, the people within it and yourself? Do you feel good about it? Do you allow relationships to develop? Or do you close the door and keep people at arm's length? I don't mean you should go round the office hugging everyone and telling them how wonderful they are – though some people do. I'm asking you to look at what happens when you meet other people. We all form first impressions, but sometimes we get it wrong and stick to those first impressions too rigidly.

Relationships often show patterns of behaviour. How are yours?

How are you in your close relationships? Do you have a pattern of difficult relationships with your boss? Do your relationships with authority show a pattern of conflict? Do you have a pattern of dysfunctional intimate relationships?

Are you putting in the time to maintain loving family relationships? Do you spend time with members of your family, supporting them and being supported by them, or is work taking up all your time? Are you too busy trying to make it today to worry about your family tomorrow?

Does your work take priority over your family? If you have one, your family is your bedrock. If you haven't any immediate close family, close friends can become the support system that a family would otherwise provide. To have a 'family' that unconditionally accepts us is important in all our lives.

I mentioned earlier that at the end of our lives we remember the times when we were involved and appreciated. There is nowhere else that you are more involved or more appreciated than within your family, whatever form it may take. For some a religious community, a military or other organisation, becomes their bedrock – and provides them with a support that they enjoy for the rest of their lives.

How is your relationship with your family and, equally importantly, how is your relationship with yourself?

## Spirit

The spirit reflects for many people their true self and defines their true purpose, and for those who are not religious, their ethical core values. Do you live by such values? Do you have good intentions? Are you honest, sincere, genuine? If you follow a spiritual path, do you do spiritual exercises, pray, go to religious services? Do you meditate and reflect upon what it is, in fact, that you are doing with your life?

A keen sense of spirit puts into meaningful perspective all other aspects of our lives.

## Career

It's important not to feel defined by the job you do, but a big part of our lives is determined by how we earn our living – our career. Have you chosen the career you wanted, or has it been chosen for you by circumstances over which you felt you had no control?

Do you have a clear goal? Does it fit in with the future that you see for yourself? Are there any unresolved issues in your current career that are causing you conflict? Are you motivated by wealth or by happiness? Is the career that you're in really the one for you?

If your career is just OK, then it may be time to think about changing it.

Finally . . .

*Wealth*
Have you thought about what wealth actually means to you? Do you know what would make you consider yourself wealthy? For some, it's having the unconditional love of family and friends throughout their lives. For others it's a precise sum of money. But I know from my personal experience that if you take care of the first six aspects in this list, the wealth will take care of itself.

So take care of your self, your health, your attitude, your relationships, your spirit, and your career – and the wealth will follow.

These are the seven aspects that you need to consider when creating your successful blueprint for the future. Add any others that for you are important. Fill in that life chart, see where you are now, and then determine what you want the chart to look like in the future.

## You the book

You've set up You Ltd. Now you have to decide what business it is that you are in. What does You Ltd stand for? What is it going to do? What are your goals for both its short- and its long-term future?

To do this you will need to write your goals and plans down in a notebook, which we'll call your life book – which is what it effectively is. You'll be able to refer back and add to the goals and plans as necessary, and they will represent your goal journey, your personal blueprint for success. This part of the procedure is similar to what I asked you to do in chapter 5, but now we're getting down to the details. And there is no better way to reinforce your goal at a subconscious level than by writing it down. It is very important that you don't shortcut this step.

All businesses start with a plan. They identify what it is they are going to do and how they are going to do it; they project income and expenditure quarterly and annually. There is no one model, of course, no one blueprint for a business plan that fits all. It's the same with your personal plan. The one you create will be the one that works best for you. It will be designed by you and understood best by you. You may wish to make your life book very chart-oriented, or you may prefer simple diary entries. It doesn't matter which – choose whichever suits you best.

The main thing is, this book is yours. The form it takes is up to you. I'll now outline the key steps that I have found to be helpful in the construction of my life book.

Choose a fresh page, and write down your list of goals. Don't worry how long the list becomes or how fanciful the goals are. The important thing is to let your brain think freely about the life goals that you want to achieve. Then look down the list and divide them into two categories: realistic goals – the ones you truly believe you can achieve; and unrealistic goals – those that you feel (or know) are beyond your physical or mental ability, or just plain impossible. For example, if you're fifty-five it's unrealistic to aim to win an Olympic gold for sprinting; if you're sixteen your aim to become a heart surgeon before you're twenty isn't likely to be realised.

Now take your list of realistic goals, and divide them into three categories: short-term (up to one month), medium-term (up to one year) and long-term (over one year and beyond). Then, taking a separate page for each, define those goals. You can have two goals or twenty running concurrently – it's up to you.

Once you have written out each page, add on each the date by which you would ideally like to achieve each goal. Now begin working backwards from this date so as to determine the stages you will need to go through. For example, if your medium-term goal is to reduce your blood pressure naturally and reduce your dependency on prescription drugs, and you would like to do this within six months, what stages will you need to go through?

First, you need to research methods of reducing blood pressure through healthy eating and exercise regimes. Find out whether there is a clinic or support organisation in your area that could help and encourage you. Decide what changes in diet you will have to make, then before you begin speak to your doctor and tell her of your intention to gradually reduce your medication so that you plan in six months' time to be controlling your blood pressure naturally. You will find, more often than not, that you will be encouraged and assisted by others in achieving your goal.

On the same sheet of paper, identify what you believe will be the problems encountered in working towards your goal. For instance, do you have a habit of giving up on things? If so, determine not to give up on this goal. Take it day by day. Perhaps you feel that you don't know enough about your new diet to confidently start on it – again, find the information you need, speak to someone who can give you some tips. Identify your problems, and don't move on until you have found a solution.

Finally, think of a picture or image or catchphrase that you can identify with the achievement of your goal. It could be a photograph of a healthier you mounted on a sheet of paper with, beneath it the words 'Low blood pressure – the new me!' It could be a written affirmation, such as 'I am getting healthier every day in my pursuit of naturally low blood pressure.' It could be a mantra that you repeat to yourself: 'I feel great on this low-blood-pressure diet!'

Keep returning to this page. You can change the plan, you can change the stages, and you can even change the completion date. But returning to this page will help you to focus your mind on exactly what it is you are trying to achieve. In summary: identify the goal, write your plan for achieving it, identify the problems and solutions, then see yourself achieving your goal through visual pictures or personal affirmations or both.

## You the movie

One of the things that are fundamental to the mind-set of winners is that they can see success before they start the journey. They can clearly visualise their goals. Before your mind can start working unconsciously to help you realise yours, you must be able to visualise them just as clearly.

I would now like to share with you the Natural Born Winner technique for effective relaxation and goal-planning through visualisation.

Before you can visualise, you must be completely and thoroughly relaxed. Make the time every morning and every evening to do this. If you need to get up early, then do so. Find a quiet room and a chair that is not too comfortable – we don't want you falling asleep! Sit upright in the chair, put your hands in your lap and breathe in through your nose very deeply for a count of five; then exhale through your mouth, slowly and gently, for a count of five. Do this eight to ten times – not too vigorously or you may get a little dizzy at first – and as you do so, say to yourself, 'I am breathing in calm. I am breathing out anger. I am breathing in energy, I am breathing out fatigue. I am breathing in relaxation, I am breathing out stress.' Make every breath a calming and soothing message to yourself. After a minute or so begin repeating slowly in your mind, 'I am relaxing, I am calm.' Let your inner-voice become fainter and fainter until it fades away completely. Pay no attention to any thoughts that come into your mind; let them go. Eventually your brain, unused to such conscious inaction, after initially seeking to distract you will become calm. At first this will be difficult to get used to, but persevere – it will happen.

The purpose of all relaxation and meditation techniques is to relax the body and still the mind. Breathing in and out in a rhythmical manner will help you to relax your body and clear your mind. Like anything worth while it takes practice, but the important thing is that you begin.

After about three or four minutes, when you are feeling completely calm, receptive and relaxed, I would like you to visualise your favourite place in the world. Think of a place you love: it might be a beach in the tropics, a street in your home town, a magical place from your childhood fantasies – whatever for you fits the description, 'favourite place in the world'.

Wherever this place is, see it in your mind's eye. If you can't see it clearly, just think about it and imagine the smells and the sounds and the feelings you associate with it. You associate joyful feelings with this place. Look around: recognise the familiar sights and experience the feelings of happiness and relaxation that go with it. What do you see? What do you smell? Is there a friend there smiling at you? Feel the comfort and security this place gives you. Feel the joyfulness, the contentment, the emotion of being there.

Now – and even if you're on a beach – I want you to imagine a pair of double doors – these form the entrance to your own private cinema. Design an entrance that you will enjoy looking at, because this will be the entrance you will 'see' every time you practise your visualisation. Now go through the double doors and walk into the foyer. Look around the foyer, and sense that you are somewhere familiar and safe. You will be in the foyer for only a short time, but feel free to let it contain anything you want – for instance, a fireplace with a roaring fire in it, or an armchair, or photographs of yourself or of your loved ones, or of friends past and present. The important thing is that you visualise a scene with strong personal connections, one that activates emotional memories.

Your passage through the foyer prepares your mind with the most positive images of well being and security. Next, you are going to enter your own private cinema to make and direct your own movie. So now walk through the foyer, towards another pair of double doors – which mysteriously and with the magic of the movies swing open in front of you. Walk down the central aisle of your cinema, and pick a wonderfully comfortable seat wherever you want.

Now the lights dim, the curtains part and on the screen appear the words 'Previous Highlights'. Project on to the screen a montage of the magical moments in your life, moments full of powerful, positive emotional memories that you will love to watch – and accompanied by your favourite music, if you like.

These memories will trigger in your mind the emotions of past successes. You may see yourself being applauded after making a speech at school; opening the envelope that contained your college acceptance; experiencing your first serious kiss; being told by someone that they love you. You may see yourself scoring a winning goal for the football team that you used to play for, or winning a business account. Whatever images you recall, they will be moments in your life when you felt totally alive. Totally successful. Totally happy.

You are feeling and recognising the emotions that accompany being a winner.

Next, the montage sequence finishes, and up on the screen comes 'Now Showing'. Look at your life as it is! See yourself as you really are, imperfections and all: see yourself sitting bored in the office; see yourself loafing around; see the aspects of your life that you don't like. Now freeze the film, and let those images fade away. Take an image of yourself biting your nails, if this is one of your least favourite habits, then look at yourself doing exactly that, then freeze the image, and let it slowly but surely fade away. See in your mind those behaviours, habits and parts of your life that you want to change and mentally see them physically disappearing from your life. You are now clearly programming your subconscious to alter those images, those things in your life that you don't like and that you really want to stop, or get rid of.

And now the lights seem to dim a little bit more, the curtain goes back further, the screen becomes bigger, the music builds and then on to the screen come the words, 'Future Presentations'. Now you are going to see yourself having achieved your goals. Now you see yourself fit and healthy, sitting behind the desk you have always dreamt of occupying, doing whatever it is that is your goal. And when you have clearly visualised this scene, float out of your seat. It's fine – you're the director, you've got a limitless budget, you can do anything you want to, so enter into the scene and become a part of it. Feel the clothes you're wearing, become a part of the scene you have created, experience the goal you have always dreamt of and emotionally connect with the feeling that goes with this success.

Make emotional memories of this future event, feel them powerfully, smell the flowers in the garden. Whatever the goal you have visualised, become a part of the film you have created of it, and move from scene to scene as if by pressing a remote-control button. When you have finished return to your seat, watch the curtains close, hear the music stop, see the lights go up. Leave the cinema quickly now, move out of the foyer and back to your beach or wherever your favourite place may be. And then slowly become aware of your present surroundings, slowly breathe in and breathe out, slowly open your eyes and come back to full awareness.

Creating such a powerful visual memory helps you to construct the goal that your mind will focus on. Going back to your written plan will further affirm it. In these ways you are powerfully reinforcing your belief in yourself. Subconsciously, the way you think of yourself, the way you act, will be profoundly affected. You will *naturally* take care of your health, your family, your career, and so on, because these things will *automatically and unconsciously* be moving in the direction of your goal.

**This is the only chance you will have on earth with this exciting adventure called life. So why not plan it and try to live it as richly, as happily, as possible?**
*Anon.*

Some may like to think that this is an irrational or even a mystical process, but in fact it is completely logical. You *can* create new goals and visualise new experiences and, at the same time, find the ability fully to relax. And as you do this more and more often, you will be able to do it more quickly. Don't worry at first if you don't see clear images (or hear the sounds you want to hear). With practice, that part of your visual memory that can create your own movies will become fully functional. And you'll be the star.

## You the sequel – to infinity and beyond!

Return daily to your visualised future. It will strengthen your focus and help you to decide whether the plan you are following really is working. If it's not, don't change the goal – change the plan. It's natural that you will experience setbacks but, whereas in the past you might have given up or seen these setbacks as confirmation of inevitable failure, now they will vanish into insignificance because you have already had that first sweet taste of success and have started to identify yourself as a winner.

Remember, this is *your* life. And your life is as valuable and meaningful as that of anyone who has ever existed on this planet. So determine to live it to the full. Live it in a way that will be an inspiration to others; make it a life that you will look back on with pride.

Today will never come again, so seize it. Don't waste time doing things that do you no good or that distance you from your dreams. Bear in mind that even your relaxation periods – *especially* your relaxation periods – are time well spent. Though others may think that you are simply sitting there, when you are visualising, you know that it is in those moments that you find your true purpose. Your life will bring you the joy and success your dream of if only you will embrace it and determine to live it to the full – to live the life you want and to achieve the goals your dream of.

**If you can dream it, you can do it.**
*Walt Disney (1901–66)*

We know that life isn't easy, that the road is long and that it will sometimes transform itself without warning into a treacherous mountain path with hairpin bends. But when you finally get to your destination, it won't be the pain or the hardship or the setbacks that you remember. It will be the satisfaction of having done what you set out to do, with the certain knowledge that a lifetime of future successes awaits you.

At the end of our lives we do not regret the things at which we failed; we regret the things we wished for and never attempted.

Return to this book and to others that have informed and inspired you: there is a wealth of information to be gleaned and so many people who can help you. Don't stand back – ask!

I can't make you a winner – you already are one. What I have tried to do is to blow away the smoke of self-doubt and fear that we all experience at some time or another in our lives.

I can wish no more for you than this – that you go on to become the natural winner that you were born to be. And of course, that you enjoy the journey. In the words of Walter Hagen, professional American golfer of the 1920s, 'Don't hurry. Don't worry. You're only here on a short visit, so don't forget to stop and smell the roses.'

# Rob's Run

It all began in Bangkok on 25 August 1986, when a beautiful child called Sumitta was born. She was blind from birth and when she was five her parents, no longer able to cope, gave her to the Pattaya orphanage. The orphanage had been started by chance in 1970 when an abandoned child was left with Father Brennan, a native of Chicago, who after his ordination in 1960 had gone to work in Thailand. The orphanage is now home to six hundred children, with schools for the blind and deaf, and a vocational training centre for disabled young adults.

In 1992 I saw an ad in a newspaper asking for people to sponsor children from the orphanage; so I decided to do my bit for charity, and was sent Sumitta's details. I arranged a monthly standing order, and that for a while was that. But my fortieth birthday was approaching, and I had decided that to celebrate the occasion I would walk from my friend Tom's remote cottage in Strathconnan in central Scotland to the remotest pub on the British mainland, the Old Forge at Inverie on the Knoydart peninsula. The distance was about seventy-three miles, and I thought it would make a suitably demanding challenge for my advancing years. So I planned and trained, and I also invited a number of colleagues to join me in what was now simply being referred to as 'the Walk'. And then I decided to use the Walk as an opportunity to raise money for Sumitta in Thailand.

I was born and raised in Glasgow, an industrial town with a big heart and a tough reputation, and as a child I always wanted to visit the Highlands and walk through the glens where long ago, I had heard, proud warriors had fought to the last man in pursuit of their freedom. At the time those glens had seemed another country, so far beyond my reach; but now I stood on the threshold of a journey that I'd dreamt about as a 'wee' boy in Glasgow thirty years before.

The big day came, and we set out. The weather was atrocious, with the rain and wind sapping our energy. When, after fourteen hellish hours, two of the party were showing signs of hypothermia, we decided to abandon the attempt.

The following year I had a second go, but a fellow hiker broke his ankle and again the trip was abandoned. Such money as I had managed to raise for Sumitta stayed in a trust account in the bank, but I still hadn't achieved my goal.

I determined to try once more, but this time nobody was available to come with me. To walk alone in such wild terrain is foolhardy and irresponsible, so things were looking bleak. A little disconsolately, on the wall of my office I put a map showing the route of the Walk, and over the next four months almost everybody who passed through the office saw the map and asked about the trip, but still no takers. Then, by great good fortune, three people offered to help me. They each brought excellent skills with them: Steve was a former Australian army instructor, Nic an Australian trainer, and Brett a South African who owned a Land Rover and who I asked to help as support driver. They all happened to be working in London, but none of them knew each other. Steve and Nic had seen the map in my office, heard about my goal, and offered immediately to support my next attempt. At the last moment my friend Chris, a doctor and former expedition physician, joined the support team.

The days building up to my third attempt had produced some of the worst weather of the year, especially up in Scotland, and it showed no sign of clearing. The day before our departure I grew increasingly anxious: a pervading sense of the previous failures hung over me. I had attempted the Walk twice before; both times the conditions had been brutal; both times I was physically exhausted by the distance and the weather; both times I had failed. I had begun to believe the Walk was an unrealistic goal. Especially now that I had set a personal goal of doing it in under forty-eight hours.

When we set out on the drive to the start point, it was windy and raining hard. Then quite unbelievably, ten miles from the start, it was as though someone had turned off the tap – the rain stopped, the clouds parted, and the sun began to shine. So at 3.30pm on Friday the 12th June 1998, I began my third attempt at the Walk.

Steve and I began the first section and Nic joined us for a night march, a demanding section of the route across a slow and treacherous peat bog. At 1.30 in the morning we reached the second planned rendezvous only to discover that the vehicle carrying the hot food had not got through. I had been going non-stop for ten hours and had covered twenty-six miles. Exhausted, we huddled together on the ground in an attempt to stay warm. After about ten minutes Steve said 'Let's go', and silently we set off into the darkness for the next rendezvous point fifteen miles away.

Six hours later we met the support vehicle. Steve and Nic rested up and promptly fell asleep. I sat down and took a look at my feet for the first time. They were not a pretty sight – four of my toenails had become detached from the nail bed. After a short rest I set off on the next six-mile section with Chris, but my feet were extremely sore and I was exhausted. After thirty painful minutes I told him I was going to quit. The whole project had been too ambitious; I had tried my best, but my feet were a mess, and I was hurting. My support walkers, too, were exhausted. Chris was very supportive of my decision, and after a while we reached the next rendezvous point by a bridge and waited for the support vehicle. Only, this time the difference was when it arrived I would be getting in. We sat there on the bridge, at the foot of the next steep mountain section, contemplating the eight-mile stretch that I was no longer willing or able to climb. Apart from the odd passing car, the silence as we sat there was complete. I gazed at my feet and dreamt of a hot bath and a long sleep.

I had by now fully justified my decision to myself, but at the same time I was disappointed. We had all given one hundred per cent, but it wasn't enough. I decided that I would have the money for Sumitta released from the trust account and sent to the orphanage; and although I had failed, I took comfort from the fact that I'd really tried.

Again, the support vehicle didn't arrive. After fifteen minutes of silence Chris gave me a serious look and quietly said 'You're going over that mountain, aren't you?' I managed to croak a tired and emotional 'Yes, I am.' 'Right then,' he replied, 'I'd better bandage up those feet of yours.'

The vehicle now arrived with Nic and Steve asleep in the back. Chris said he was too tired to make the climb with me, but Brett the driver announced that he would come, even though he was only wearing street shoes. We hiked over the steep section and four hours later, after twenty-two and a half hours and fifty-five miles we reached Kinloch Hourn, the overnight resting-place.

The next day, rested, refreshed and with freshly bandaged feet, I walked with Chris, Nic and Steve the final eighteen miles. I arrived forty-six hours and twenty-two minutes after leaving the starting-point. I had covered seventy-three miles. I'd done it. I walked into the Old Forge pub and ordered a pint of Guinness. And then Chris asked me to explain why I had gone on after I had so adamantly decided to give up.

I told him that as we'd walked on through the night, Nic and I had discovered that we shared not only a movie we had both enjoyed – *Braveheart* – but also the sentiment of our favourite scene from that movie. The scene is about the eve of the first battle that the Scots faced against the superior English army. William Wallace comes upon some Scottish soldiers who are running away. He asks them why. 'Because if we run we'll live, and if we stay we may die,' comes the reply. To which Wallace replies, 'Fight and you may die, run and you'll live – for a while. And dying in your beds many years from now, would you be willing to trade all the days from this day to that for one chance, just once chance, to come back here and tell our enemies that they may take our lives, but they'll never take our freedom?'

As I'd sat on that bridge exhausted and dejected, I'd thought about the strangers, now my companions, who had seen the map on my office wall and had given of their time to support my dream, and I'd thought of the miraculous lift in the weather. But most of all I'd thought of Sumitta: I had promised myself I would actively raise money for her.

I thought then, what would I give, one year from now, to come back and have this chance again? I had been looking for reasons to quit, not reasons to keep going. I remembered that the winner is simply someone who gets up one more time than they fall over. I know we all have the ability to dig a little deeper, persevere a little longer, and in my temporary discomfort I had been seeking to take the easy option. To keep going was no longer a hardship, it was a privilege.

The next day, less than one hour after we left Knoydart, it clouded over and the storm weather returned.

One last thing. If you should ever wish to take on the Walk, when you arrive at the Old Forge pub in Inverie you will find a plaque on the wall in the bar that commemorates 'Rob's Run', and there's money behind the bar for a pint of Guinness. It's on me and Sumitta. Leave a drink behind the bar for the next person, and take away with you a good thought for your hopes and dreams.

# Suggested Reading

Canfield, Jack, and Mark Victor Hansen, *Chicken Soup for the Soul* (series) Vermilion, Random House UK.

Canfield, Jack and Jacqueline Miller, *Heart at Work*, McGraw Hill, USA

de Mello, Tony, *The Prayer of the Frog*, Image Books, UK

Fenchuk, Gary W., *Timeless Wisdom*, Cake Eaters Inc., USA

Fisher, Mark, *The Instant Millionaire*, Hammond Books, UK

Gross, Daniel, *Forbes' Greatest Business Stories of All Time*, John Wiley & Son, USA

Hill, Napoleon, *Think and Grow Rich*, Fawcett Crest, USA

Maltz, Maxwell, *Psycho-Cybernetics*, Wiltshire Books, USA

Morris, Tom, *True Success*, Piatkus, UK

Peale, Norman Vincent, *The Power of Positive Thinking*, Cedar Press, USA

Weil, Andrew, *Eight Weeks to Optimum Health*, Warner Books, USA

For a full range of information on the Sieger Group's public seminars, consulting services and business training courses, please contact

The Sieger Group
123 Wakehurst Road
London SW11 6BZ
0800 917 2938

www.siegergroup.com
robin@siegergroup.com